Gifted Children

GIFTED CHILDREN

Recognising and Developing Exceptional Ability

MARGARET BRANCH

AND

AUBREY CASH

With a Preface by
PROF. JOSEPH A. LAUWERYS
D.Sc., D.Lit., F.R.I.C.

SOUVENIR PRESS

First published 1966 by Souvenir Press
Ltd., 95 Mortimer Street, London, W.1,
and simultaneously in Canada by
The Ryerson Press, Toronto 2, Canada

*Printed in Great Britain at
The Central Press, Aberdeen*

" *While all of you in the City are brothers, we will say in our tale, yet God in fashioning those of you who are fitted to hold rule mingled gold in their generation, for which reason they are the more precious* "

Plato—THE REPUBLIC

Acknowledgements

Although much excellent work is being done in this country concerning the recognition and education, in the fullest sense, of gifted children, there is an important drawback—a lack of communication between the various groups of educationalists and others engaged in the work.

This made it necessary for the authors to depend on random samples only, although they did follow every lead they were given. If they have missed any outstanding piece of work in this field, they can only tender their apologies and ask readers to contact them through the publishers so that corrections can be made in later editions.

They are especially indebted to the many parents and children who willingly spoke to them and without whose co-operation much of this book could not have been written.

Grateful thanks are due to the author of the preface, Professor J. A. Lauwerys, of the London University Institute of Education. As co-editor of the *Yearbooks of Education*, he is one of the people most responsible for the growing concern with the needs of gifted children.

The authors also wish to thank the following:

Lady Agnew, M.A., Headmistress Royal Ballet School; Dottore Roberto Assagioli, Presidente dell' Instituo di Psicontesi, Florence; Mrs. P. M. Bailey, M.A., Principal Lecturer Maria Grey Training College; Dr. A. D. Bannatyne, Ph.D.; Anthony Brackenbury, Esq., M.A., Headmaster Yehudi Menuhin School; Dr. S. A. Bridges, Ph.D., Senior Lecturer Brentwood Training College; Mrs. A. Butler, M.A., Philippa Fawcett Training College; Dr. C. M. Fleming, M.A., Ed.B., Ph.D., formerly Reader in Education,

London University; Frank Foster, Esq., Borstal After-Care Association; Sir Arnold Haskell, C.B.E., Director Royal Ballet School; Professor O. S. Heyns, Professor of Obstetrics and Gynaecology, University of Witwatersrand, South Africa; Miss Irene Hilton, M.Sc.; Mlle. Aniela Jaffé; Robert Kirby, Esq.; George Lyward, Esq., M.A., Headmaster Finchden Manor; Yehudi Menuhin, Esq.; Eric Miller, Esq.; Miss Ursula Moreton, Ballet Principal Royal Ballet School; T. L. Morgan, Esq., M.Sc., Principal Southend College of Technology; Robin Pedley, Esq., M.A., Director Institute of Education, Exeter; George Robb, Esq., M.A., Senior Psychologist Essex Education Committee; Otto L. Shaw, Esq., Headmaster Redhill School for Maladjusted Boys; Dr. Shipp, M.A., Ph.D., D.I.C., A.M.I.Chem.E., Brunel College of Advanced Technology; Dr. David Stafford-Clark, M.D., F.R.C.S., D.P.M., Physician in Charge, Dept. of Psychological Medicine, Guy's Hospital; Mrs. Moira Steel, Advisory Service for Education; Dr. C. P. Stevens, M.B.E., M.B., Ch.B., Director Spastics Society; Prof. D. H. Stott, M.A., Ph.D., Dept. of Psychology, Glasgow University; G. T. C. Tudor, Esq., M.A., Headmaster De La Rue School for Spastics; Dr. Warne of the Swedish Institute, London; D. B. Bartlett, Esq., M.A., Chief Education Officer Southend County Borough; J. L. Longland, Esq., M.A., Chief Education Officer Derbyshire County Council.

Also the following Heads of Schools:

George Appleton, Esq.; Hubert and Lois Childs; Robert Heppel, Esq.; R. S. O. Meyer, Esq.; Miss McLeod; J. M. E. Stokes; Miss Turner; D. C. W. Waters, Esq.

M. BRANCH
A. CASH

Contents

===

Illustrations

═══

Preface

IT is often thought that highly intelligent and gifted children always have an easy time and a happy life. Quickly recognised by teachers and praised by them, they sail through examinations, their various names appear on Honours Boards, employers compete to pay them large salaries, they move through brilliant careers to positions of power and privilege.

Alas, the opposite is often true. They may irritate their parents as much as they do their teachers, they may have to hide their brilliance in order to avoid trouble, the subject matter as well as the style of ordinary examinations—stressing as they must docility and conformity—may repel them. Their total experience of life, school and work may lead to frustration, disappointment, deformation, unhappiness.

Evidently, teachers need to know much more about giftedness, high ability, unusual talent, excellence—in short, about a kind of genius, about the two percent. who have it in them to contribute to culture, science and civilisation by advancing the arts and the technologies. How do such unusual people grow and develop? How can their gifts be nourished? What sort of schools and what sort of teaching will encourage, not thwart them?

Enquiries may help us to get clearer ideas; and in the first place, we shall have to learn what questions to ask. True, there is already a rich literature available, much of it—from Terman onwards—contributed by educational psychologists of goodwill and insight. Yet, to some degree, the investigations and results described tend to accept assumptions implicit in present day organisations; i.e., technological societies depending upon mass industries which imply conformity and standardisation, docility and acceptance. As a result, their measurements and evaluations lie within the grooves of convention, whereas individual genius often tries to break through them. Secondly, the importance of the emotional and fantasy life of the young is often minimised—yet it is precisely here that clues

13

may be found. Thirdly, usually implicitly, heredity is magnified, environment minimised. Professor Fred Hoyle, in one of his science fiction entertainments, defends with a measure of seriousness the hypothesis that genius is a lucky accident, like winning a prize in a football pool and, therefore, equally rare. Those who from the beginning acquire the right learning habits go from strength to strength; those who acquire the wrong are segregated to the E.S.N. classes. Hoyle, of course, goes too far! And yet. . . . What *would* happen if the right educational regimen, right for every individual, could be provided?

There are two main reasons why we should endeavour to adjust our offerings so as to promote the development of the gifted. First, quite simply in order to diminish unhappiness and frustration. Secondly, because in this last third of the twentieth century mankind needs, very badly and urgently, the contribution of the gifted to the advancement of human welfare and to the improvement of societies.

The present book describes experiments in the education of the specially gifted. It makes no claim to deep scholarship, nor is it intended as a definitive contribution based upon statistically valid test procedures. It is simply an exploration, an investigation, an account of imaginative attempts to deal sympathetically with problems as they arise. Where theoretical interpretations are offered, they are no more than tentative. They tell in popular language how, in some cases, talented children have been helped to realise their potential.

We welcome this entertaining, pleasant and modest book which, in many ways, breaks new ground. It will help teachers and parents by explaining what has been done and what can be done to encourage the flowering of talent. Many of us regret that although much is being done in this country and elsewhere to discover ways of helping the gifted to work at the top of their bent, there is no certain way in which those engaged in such work can get to know what colleagues are doing. Here, too, the present book will be useful : it will encourage research and support the activities of the recently founded Association for Gifted Children. May it have the wide circulation and success it so richly deserves.

J. A. LAUWERYS

1

The Right to be a Child

IN a Law Report of 1850, the following exchange is recorded between Judge and Defendant, the latter no more than a child:

Alderman: Do you know what an Oath is?

Boy: No.

Alderman: Do you say your prayers?

Boy: No.

Alderman: Do you know what God is?

Boy: No.

Alderman: What *do* you know?

Boy: I knows how to sweep a crossing.

Alderman: And that's all?

Boy: That's all. I sweeps a crossing.

The old order may give way to the new but it takes an unconscionably long time to do so. It was about a hundred years prior to the above incident that Rousseau was writing (in his book " Emile " published in 1762) "We know nothing of childhood, and with our mistaken notion, the further we advance, the further we go astray. The wisest writers devote themselves to what a man ought to know without asking what a child is capable of learning. They are always looking for the man in the child, without considering what he is before he becomes a man."

True enough, the young crossing sweeper was a victim of his class and, at his age, the children of well-to-do parents were still at school. But were these " privileged " children any better off, other than in the material sense? At this point, the authors want to make clear their belief that the majority of people—unlike the lady in the revue sketch who, rather than be poor and happy, prefers to

be a " misery in mink "—prefer to be both happy and rich! To
be the child of wealthy parents, up to less than a hundred years
ago, implied strictures of upbringing, both at home and at school,
which hardly allowed for any real childhood in the broadest sense
of the word. In their respective ways, the youthful crossing sweeper
and the upper-middle-class schoolboy were denied the right to be
a child.

It is, nevertheless, interesting to realize that the myth of happy
childhood is essential to adults, as a form of escape from the even
greater frustrations of being an adult . . . " Happy those early
days when I shined in my angel infancy " wrote Henry Vaughan,
the 17th Century poet, exemplifying the tendency of mortals to
take refuge in fantasies of golden childhood days, the days when
the sun shone perpetually and all was full of love and totally
lacking in the complexity of being alive.

We need to believe in a time of such happiness and this may
well be one of the reasons why it was so easy to forget the very
real misery, for so many, of being a child at a time when childhood
was one long period of disregard, deprivation and almost total
misunderstanding. It is such a defence which helps to slow down
any effort that can be made to gain knowledge, and therefore
improve conditions by a growing awareness of the harsh reality of
any situation. We had to wait for Freud before we could fully
relate the cause of adult inadequacy to the confusions and disturbances of childhood.

" Nature wants children to be children before they are men.
If we deliberately pervert this order, we shall get premature fruits
which are neither ripe nor well-flavoured and which soon decay
. . . childhood has ways of seeing, thinking and feeling peculiar
to itself; nothing can be more foolish than to substitute our ways
for them." This further quotation from Rousseau would seem to
confirm that it was he who was initially responsible for so fully
promulgating an awareness of the climate of childhood. Unfortunately, he was no less guilty than Vaughan of the " crime " of
false recall. He too believed in the innocence of childhood and
felt that such innocence should be preserved and that " true
education is simply the education of the original nature of the

child." Rousseau was as mistaken in his need to consider all child-hood as beatific as Calvin was in taking the opposite view.

In England, the growing awareness of the condition of childhood, as such, might be said to have been triggered off by the realization that one section of it was being subjected to degrees of brutality that even an adult should not have to tolerate; and the credit for this realization can be laid at the door of popular novelists, such as Dickens and Charles Kingsley, especially, the latter in his immortal book *The Water Babies*. The prosperity resulting from the Industrial Revolution was, perversely, making it possible for children to work in conditions that crippled them for life, emotion-ally and physically. The under-privileged poor were, for the first time, beginning to be the centre of public concern.

In the report of the Commission on the Employment of Young Persons and Children (1842) a girl of eight said: " I'm a trapper in the Gamber pit. I have to trap without a light, and I'm scared. I never go to sleep. Sometimes I sing when I have a light, but not in the dark; I dare not sing then." The conditions under which the children worked in the mines were certainly not exaggerated by those writing the report . . . " Chained, belted like dogs in a go-cart, saturated, and more than half-naked, crawling upon their hands and feet and dragging their heavy loads behind them, they present an appearance indescribably disgusting and unnatural."

Disraeli went to see for himself what the conditions were like and, in his novel *Sybil*, gives us a picture of the effect of these conditions on a boy, Dandy Mick, a young tough of sixteen years . . . " with a lithe figure and a handsome, faded, impudent face." A middle-aged woman, Mother Carey, is shocked because he expresses no grief for his dying mother (Victorian novelists were nearly all under the impression that death brought out the good in people). Dandy Mick's attitude, however, is far more realistic. " That's a good one," he said, " I should like to know what my mother ever did for me but give me treacle and laudanum when I was a baby to stop my tongue and fill my stomach."

Thus a juvenile delinquent of our own time might talk (but in a more contemporary idiom of course) forced by circumstances into a degree of egocentricity, which allowed not at all for the possibility of any constructive relationships, convinced that the world owed him a living, and that no one had ever attempted to help him. Poverty and deprivation, like death, are certainly not the ennobling factors in children's lives that they were once thought to be.

Today, deprived children do better from the physical point of view, but there are more ways of being deprived than one, deprived indeed of being a child at all.

Even in times of ignorance, there have been pockets of enlightenment, so it is that during the early 19th Century, we have the case of Pestolozzi, the Swiss educationalist, who was given the job of looking after a group of children orphaned during the Napoleonic wars. His was one of the very first attempts to study children, *qua* children, and his work, handed down to followers, has continued ever since. After the 2nd World War, Pestolozzi Village was set up in Switzerland, where children from every combatant country were given a chance to grow together and learn together, and perhaps form a truly international community. While there continue to be wars, children will continue to arrive, and people the Village. They live in houses with a house mother and father of their own nationality, but schooling is communal and students from all over the world spend part of their Summer vacation helping in the Village. A branch of this Village has been established in England (Sussex).

A revolution in education and thinking with regard to children in general has occurred since Dr. Arnold, famous Headmaster of Rugby, said in the middle of the 19th Century, in an address to his scholars that " what we must look for here is, first, religious and moral principles, second, gentlemanly conduct and, thirdly, intellectual ability." Arnold was considered something of a pioneer in his day. At least he realized that in order to take responsibility, one had to be trained for it, and it was he who instituted the prefectorial system which, for all the fact that it was much abused at the time, genuinely attempted to cope with the real brutality which had gone on among the sons of " gentlemen." Nevertheless, more than fifty years later, the cult of cerebration to the exclusion of assimilation could still prove that we were failing to understand children. What prefectorial system could have been devised to make the lot easier of Dr. Norbert Wiener, the American scientist, famous for his work on cybernetics, and who died in 1964?

Dr. Wiener was a highly gifted child who started to read when he was three years old, went to College at the age of eleven, graduated with Honours when he was fourteen, gained his Ph.D. in Mathematical Logic when he was eighteen and then went to Cambridge, and he later worked at the Massachusetts Institute of Technology.

He always looked back to his childhood as a period of great isolation and unhappiness. Of his fellow pupils in College, he said that they were mostly seven years older than himself, and seemed fully grown adults and that the seats were much too big for him. For some of the lessons, he had to sit on the teacher's lap.

When he entered University at the age of twelve, he felt more out of place than ever. " A deep estrangement fell upon me, which has made me feel all my life a sojourner on this planet, rather than a native . . . I had to create for myself a fantastic personality and become an actor in real life. Only then could I adapt myself to the various parts I was called on to fulfil." It is not easy for a highly gifted child to feel at home in a world which does not fully understand him, and therefore cannot accept him.

The case of Dr. Wiener can be taken as a warning that even when a child is recognized for its true worth, it is still possible for damage to occur if it is not catered for *entirely*. We shall be concerned, in this book, mainly with the recognition and proper treatment of the gifted, and proper treatment applies to realms other than intellectual. It is simply not enough for a gifted child to be placed all the time with his intellectual equals, as is sometimes the case in America. This leads, as it must, to a cult of an élite, and these children will not always have the protection that their School offers. The time will come when they are let loose in the world as human beings, and as human beings they will be failures, over-cerebrally inclined, donnish in the worst sense of the word, and with the unlikeableness that their feeling of superiority creates.

The breeze of change suddenly became a wind when, in France, Charcot studied the basis of hysteria in adults and passed on his new insight to Freud. But it was Freud who took the next step and postulated that neurotic behaviour in later life stemmed directly from childhood, both from the external events that take place in the child's life, and, much more important, the things that had occurred internally in the formation of his personality. A great step forwards had been taken in understanding children, and therefore making the need apparent for the provision of conditions under which they would most likely develop into healthy and happy human beings. Through the study of sickness, we learnt to provide the climate for health, both socially and psychologically.

With the new and growing awareness of the child and his world, it is not surprising that leaders of psychological thought began to consider various refinements of this " new " field of investigation. One such refinement of consideration was the very special internal world of the highly intelligent child, the world, for instance, of the youthful Carl Jung.

Jung never forgot how intensely lonely he felt during his childhood. How, because he could find no one with whom to talk over the questions of love and hate and sin and redemption which really interested him, he settled for being a typical schoolboy about whom the teacher said to his father—" He's just average, but he works commendably hard." One day, however, an event occurred which made a profound impression on Jung. The class were set a composition which, for once, was of interest to him. The fifteen-year-old boy set to work, fired by enthusiasm and turned in a piece of work for which he confidently expected good marks. When the essays were returned, the master commented on all the others and then turned to him. " Now I have one more composition . . . Jung's. It is by far the best, and I ought to have given it first place. Unfortunately it is a fraud! Where did you copy it from? Confess the truth!! "

The boy was shocked, both by the fact that he had been accused of cheating and, most of all, by the fact that the teacher had not thought him capable of doing work of this standard. He protested, but it did no good. The other pupils also thought he had cheated. He became disheartened and bitter about the whole thing. What was the good of trying to explain himself? Suddenly he came to terms with himself, and at the same time took a great step forward in not only understanding his own predicament, but the over-all predicament of the gifted child. " What is really going on here?" he asked himself. " All right, you are excited and upset. Of course the teacher is an idiot who doesn't understand your nature—he doesn't understand it any more than you do. Therefore he is as mistrustful as you are. You mistrust yourself and others, that is why you side with those who are naïve and simple and easily seen through. One gets excited when one doesn't understand things." Such internal observations at the age of fifteen might well have been responsible for the very basis of his life's work with his patients, for until the day he died, he was always asking " what is really going on there? "

Jung, like all children, had a desperate need for acceptance by his peer group and only by playing down his intelligence could he hope to get this. By itself, this isolation from his less gifted contemporaries should have been enough to contend with, but such a refusal on the part of his teacher to accept his brilliance amounts to a classic example of the refusal of the right to be a brilliant child! The opposite, one could say, of Dr. Norbert Wiener.

The needs of children, indeed, would seem to be boundless and of a complexity that cannot be calculated. There can never be enough work done in the attempt to make their development reach its potential, and the field of investigation, widening further as the end of the 19th Century rolled nearer, was enriched by Frederick Fröbel, from Bavaria, whose work even today remains an inspiration.

In America, ideas about children and the way they might be educated, were simmering in the minds of psychologists and teachers alike during the years prior to the turn of the 20th Century, and pioneer work was done at Harvard and Johns Hopkins Universities. In 1882, John Dewey set up a " psychological laboratory " and in 1896 the Laboratory School, where children, and methods of teaching them, could be studied. The methods were not nearly as cold-blooded as the use of the word

" laboratory " suggests, for this was a time when scientific jargon was greatly in vogue. But it was not until some thirty years later that the concept of the " Child Centred School " was developed in the form which we know it today.

In 1914, Stanely Hall, an American psychologist, wrote one of the first books ever to be written about adolescents. This was the first clear piece of thinking about this particular age group and, since then, there has been an avalanche of literature on this group, but no more than necessary for today's adolescent dominated society. In the 1920's, Terman began his studies of gifted children in America and, in England, Susan Isaacs studied the children at the Malting House School for young children, a high proportion of whom were exceptionally intelligent as they were the sons and daughters of Cambridge dons.

The thought and research continues, and at last we have some idea of what children are like, although the question of catering for the gifted child still remains a problem, more pressing today than ever, for we as a nation cannot afford to waste even one of them.

Children, considered as a class with its own special requirements, needing its own laws, and demanding its own recognition, have come to stay.

2

What is a Gifted Child?

"THE first duty which the Gods have placed upon rulers is to scrutinize every child from birth and see what kind of metal enters into the composition of their souls. They are then to select all children of Gold, whether they come from parents of Gold, or as may occasionally happen, from parents of silver or even bronze." Thus wrote Plato in " The Republic."

This placed an onus of responsibility upon the rulers which, one has to assume, might well have made them want to relinquish their position! What ruler, past or present, is equipped to recognize " Golden children " in ways that could guarantee the rightness of such selection?

Golden children are not always easy to recognize. " The gifted child is one who is consistently superior in any worthwhile line of endeavour " wrote Professor Paul Witty. But the complexities of human nature are such that a thousand and one reasons can be found for a failure of consistency, and just as many reasons for a general inability to use one's intelligence to any constructive end whatsoever. The story of Peter (see the chapter on Maladjustment) is a case in point.

But the time of Plato was less complex than ours. Nowadays, having assessed the level of brilliance in a child who seems incapable of employing it, we look to the " rulers " to make it possible for modern physical and psychiatric methods to be brought to bear, in order that potentiality may be achieved. Children, apparently, of bronze, can be turned into children of gold, and so far as the authors are concerned, gold, even potential gold, is high intelligence (intelligence that registers in the I.Q. scale at 135 and over) or outstanding creativity.

An immense amount of money has, quite rightly, been spent in recent years to try to help the disabled child, such as the spastic, suffering from cerebral palsy due to brain damage, other physically handicapped groups, or the mentally retarded. Nevertheless, up to twenty-five years ago, and even today in some parts of the country, if a child were found to be mentally backward, and the education authorities felt he would benefit from special schooling, the parents were often reluctant to let him go to such an institution, fearing the suggestion of stigma. However, the climate is gradually changing and parents are beginning to realize that it is better for such a child to go to a school where teachers have had an extra year's training. Here the child stays, by law, until he is sixteen, where the classes never comprise more than twenty pupils . . . better this than allowing the child to flounder at the bottom of a class of forty or more children of his own age group, where he learns nothing, and becomes even more discouraged than necessary.

It is an achievement that we have at long last recognized the necessity for the specialized handling of handicapped children . . . but so far we are comparatively ignorant of the needs of that vital two percent. of the population, the child who is gifted.

Such children are the gold of their country and it is our duty to protect this potential mental wealth by recognizing the value of their brilliance, helping to develop their gifts in such a way that they become whole and happy human beings, protecting them too from the rejection, frustration and generally unwise handling that would seem to be the lot of many children of high intelligence.

Gifted children are in a class of their own. Like a sensitive and precision-made machine, they need to be treated with exceptional care, and a respect for the delicate intricacies which constitute their make-up; and like such a machine, unwise or incorrect handling will not only produce below par results, but may cause irreparable damage.

Intelligence is assessed by the use of the I.Q. These two potent letters occasionally have the same effect on people as did the word " culture " on Göring—they reach for their guns. But, by and large, intelligence quotient tables are a useful guide, along with other methods, not only to basic capacity, but also to potential achievement, although many of the reasons resulting in a dichotomy between capability and achievement are, in fact, dealt with in this book.

Sir Francis Galton was the first to attempt the investigation of intelligence through the use of an empirically acquired " norm " of achievement. He found that all men of outstanding ability had certain common characteristics which he defined as (a) ability (b) zeal and (c) a readiness to work. He thought these characteristics derived from inheritance and, indeed, called his book, published in 1869, *Hereditary Genius*. His contention was that those of outstanding ability differed from the rest only in degree, but not in kind. But he did believe that two kinds of ability existed, that which was general, and that which was specialized and indicated a basic aptitude.

" Without a special gift for mathematics, a man cannot be a mathematician, but without a high degree of general ability, he will never make a great mathematician " wrote Galton, and nearly a hundred years later, we get Sir Arnold Haskell's view, when selecting children for the Royal Ballet School, that a child may be a gifted dancer and, from the physical point of view, the ideal shape, but she or he will never be a great dancer unless she is also of above average intelligence. So although psychological thinking develops continually, Galton's premise cannot, even now, be wholly rejected.

Alfred Binet knew of the work undertaken by Galton and he too realized that there must be some way of grouping children according to their abilities, and not according to their scholastic attainments. He devised a scale that took into account only knowledge acquired by a child from the basic experience of living, and found that intelligence was not only inherited, but innate. In the process, a multitude of French children were tested, including his own, and the results compared.

This is still the standard method. Thousands of children of approximately the same background and age are tested. We find that out of a thousand children, half fall in the middle of the scale, and the rest to one or other side of the halfway line. Taking the middle of the line as 100, some children will score 140 and over (these are the gifted) and others between 50 and 70 (the educationally sub-normal).

The educationally sub-normal can go to special schools where teachers are specially trained to deal with them, where classes are much smaller, and where the children are required to spend a year more than usual, for their rate of learning is slow.

Even further down the scale are those who need special care outside the educational system. There are also those children, of varying intelligence, who may be physically or emotionally handicapped—the blind, the spastic, the maladjusted. All of these children are catered for, but what about the fit?

Why should the fit be catered for? Perhaps we can suggest an analogy. A man falls off a motor-bike and lies in the road, injured. A crowd gathers round, involved in the injured man's predicament for a variety of reasons, morbid, sympathetic or merely curious. But the victim will be helped—people have allowed themselves to be involved. Another man will be walking around a city, lonely, dissatisfied and unrecognized. Presumably he is fit, so nobody worries. Yet he is in a rut, and he cannot escape from it by himself. His condition prevents him from contributing anything constructive and he is as helpless as a child. Should he be blamed, or should he be helped?

The gifted child can just as easily be " lost." He too must be catered for, and there is a growing awareness of his needs.

Returning to the assessment of intelligence, this is achieved by dividing a child's mental age (his score on the intelligence test) by his age in months (his chronological age) and multiplying the result by 100. Thus a child of six years who scores as high as a child of nine would, in fact, have an intelligence quotient of 150 and thus come into the category of the gifted. Alternatively, a six years old whose score was no more than that of a child of three, would have an I.Q. of 50, and thus be classed as sub-normal.

Since 1911 there have been many revisions of Binet's test. The first major one was made at Stanford University, in the U.S.A., in the early twenties and named the Stanford Binet test. It is still in use today as an individual test, but the most common tests in use in British schools today are the Group Tests. These can be given to a group of children by the teacher who, although she follows the printed instructions, has not been psychologically trained in testing. The tests are on a printed form and the children follow printed instructions, so must be able to read and write with some ease. No measuring instrument is quite perfect and when a really fine assessment is needed, person to person tests are given by a trained and experienced psychologist. This " battery " of tests, as they are referred to, give a far more accurate idea of the child's capabilities.

Because all tests need to be standardized, they must be made as reliable an instrument as possible so, in the case of group tests, each time a new one is devised, it is distributed among education authorities all over the country in order that children of widely differing backgrounds, but of the same age at the time the test is given, can complete them. Teachers are asked to make their comments and to seek ambiguities such as the use of the word " starved," for to a London child to be starved is to be very hungry, but to be " starved " in the West Riding of Yorkshire could also mean to be very cold. The results of these tests are studied, revisions made and only then are they considered standardized and ready for use.

These tests are, occasionally, criticized for their failure to reveal special aptitudes and in America, de Haan and Havighurst say that mental ability has various components such as " verbal skill, spatial imagination, science, mathematics, art, music, social leadership " and so on, thus by this definition, a gifted child must come well above his age level in more than one of these groups. The common denominator in all these controversial views, however, is the awareness of more than one kind of intelligence, and the belief that the gifted not only acquire exceptional knowledge, but make exceptional use of it.

To the late Professor Lewis Terman of Stanford University, gifted children were of life-long and absorbing concern. It was under his jurisdiction that the Stanford revisions of Binet's tests were devised, and as early as 1907 he wrote the thesis on which he was awarded his doctorate, comparing seven dull children with seven highly intelligent children. He gained world recognition from his study of " A Thousand Gifted Children " in 1925, and follow up studies have been done on these same subjects ever since, following their development into adults, and their comparative achievements, although Terman himself died in 1956.

Terman found that the gifted child nearly always manifested his talents early, providing the parents were sufficiently aware to note the signs. Thus he realized the necessity, and insisted upon it, for close contact between investigator, educator and parent.

Consequently, the parents were made very aware of the " golden child " in their midst, and were able to note the difference between their child, and the children of other parents. The " golden " ones were quick to grasp new ideas, very active, showed desire to learn and to know, had exceptionally good memories for both facts and events, and were unusually mature in their conversation. This gift for conversation can easily be repressed. If a child is considered " cocky " and consistently slapped down, he will give up trying to talk about the things that interest him.

There was, also, ease and rapidity of learning at school (always providing the lessons were not below the level of stimulation they needed), an unusual concern with what went on in their world, and a tendency to ask far more questions needing a far greater diversity of answers, than did other children.

Gifted children talk early but, more striking, grasp the essential meaning of words and use them correctly. In his studies, Terman discovered that such children averaged a vocabulary of more than twenty-five words at eighteen months, and that two of them learned to read before they were three years old while many were able to read before they were four!

It is important to realize that this ability to learn when so young is something more than a normal ability accomplished in less than normal time. It suggests an unusual percipience in the child, an ability to grasp the essential meaning of a situation even with the most limited contact with this very situation. So much so, that a gifted child is often thought to have an indifferent nature—he turns so quickly away from things. In point of fact, he has grasped the essentials so quickly that there is no further need for concentration.

There is also an unusual capacity for retention and for using knowledge acquired in a completely new situation, in other words, the early ability to exploit their own knowledge. Most very young children are bewildered by something new, but to the gifted child, something new is something stimulating, and to be compared with impressions stored from previous experience. Such a child, taken shall we say, to a wedding, rather than being confused and over-excited with the bustle and activity and demands upon his good behaviour, will be constantly " with it " to the extent of noting, and perhaps indiscreetly repeating, an overheard and bitchy remark! Pas devant this particular enfant indeed!

Another attribute of the gifted child is an unusual awareness of the relationship between one thing and another. At the age of six, Nancy was given the Stanford Binet test questions for a child aged eleven, and answered them with ease, especially those needing this grasp of relationship—" A snake, a cow and a sparrow are alike because they are all alive; they are different because they move differently; " " a rose, a potato and a tree are all plants that grow from the ground." However, she also wrote "A knifeblade, a penny and wire are all made of different stuff like iron, but it is the same too, only I can't think of the name." The gifted are not gifted all of the time, and such evidence of very human failure is reassuring. We should not be anxious to produce a race of intellectual monsters.

Two main ways, then, make it possible for gifted children to be discovered, (a) general observation and (b) testing. In the former the parents are of primary importance, and it is essential that they be acquainted with the new discoveries relating to intelligence in the young. Unless such children are " discovered " early, they will not be handled correctly and, as we have said, may easily be damaged for they, so much more than children of average intelligence, have a basic need for making good personal relationships within the home, in order to help them withstand the rejection by their own age group, which may well follow.

Given this emotional security, the next step is to safeguard their health, and then the concern should be, for instance, to see that they have access to the kind of reading they prefer, which encompasses a wider range than obtainable from many "Children's libraries," to encourage, also, any interest in art and music (and if gifted in these directions, to see that expert opinion is obtained in order that the best possible training can be given from the start, obviating the need to "unlearn" at a later stage).

The stimulus of travel is needed, even if no more than a school journey to Brighton. This, and other forms of stimulation, the parent can provide to a greater or less degree, but the most important thing of all, is for the parent to respect the child to the extent of allowing it to be itself, and not to live vicariously through it. So often parents who have, themselves, failed in life, are too possessive about their gifted children, wishing to act out their own unfulfilled ambitions through them, and in the process driving the child beyond its capacity. This very special problem is dealt with in a later chapter.

Finally, we suggest that most gifted children come under the following categories:

1. Of very high intelligence, I.Q. 140+ revealed on testing, interested in abstract ideas and principles, enjoying learning from books. Able to marshall their thoughts and draw conclusions from what they have learned.

2. Of equally high intelligence, but preferring to deal with the concrete solution of problems, a liking to make things with their hands, inventive, an ability to construct their own apparatus.

3. Creative, also above normal I.Q. but with some special ability, especially in the arts (but not in painting. Early achievement in this is common and can disappear).

4. Of high intelligence coupled with social maturity, and the ability to get on with their fellows without sacrificing their own ideas. Unlike those in the first three categories, they do not attempt to over-organize their disciples, and perhaps for this very reason they tend to elect them as their leaders, respecting their authority, yet not feeling threatened by their (probably discreetly concealed) exceptional aptitudes.

3

Little Lamb who made Thee?

WHEN Patricia was a child, her grandfather realized that she was gifted, and hoped she would be allowed to realize her potential. Her mother, however, had fixed ideas about how a girl should go through life. A girl should be interested in pretty clothes, a girl should go to parties to meet a nice boy, and then a girl should get married. Patricia, however, was far more interested in staying at school, but the University education she longed for was denied her. She had to wait until she was married before the gifts she had inherited could be used to their best advantage—to bring up her own gifted children in the wholly enlightened way that, as a child, she had longed for.

"It's difficult to remember when I realized that my own son (Peter) was gifted. It was during the war and I was living in total isolation with him and therefore I had all the time in the world to spend with him and on him. I first noticed my own deficiencies and, perhaps therefore, his gifts when he was two and a half or three. He started asking me the various instruments in a very big orchestra that I could not name. I realized that I had something on my hands that I could not deal with.

"It wasn't that he was particularly fond of music; he was fond of everything and by the time he was three he knew everything that I knew more or less. Already he could read and write perfectly, and seemed to know the name of every wild flower in the country. He was always saying 'Mummy read me a story' and that's why I taught him. Then it was 'Mummy may I read you a story?'

"He was already walking at about nine months, and nine months later he was talking, but he always was very co-ordinated

physically. My daughter (Helen) isn't, though she certainly has a
mind. Peter would throw and catch balls quite accurately. If I
went swimming he had to go on my back as I had no-one to leave
him with, so too with riding. He had to come. He enjoyed it. I
don't remember his having any early fears, not even of the dark.
Both children always talked in their most open way after ' lights
out.'

" He was always asking questions about anything and everything. For instance, at three and a half I started him at a Convent
School, and his first question was ' Don't Nuns have legs? '
Within three days it was ' Mummy they do! ' Questions were
everlasting and on everything, but I had all the time in the world
with him as my husband was in the Army during the war and
didn't come home for three years. Peter and I developed a kind
of animal telepathic instinct with each other. All children are born
with this but it gets lost in the problems of growing up. If we were
going out somewhere in the afternoon, on that morning Peter
would tell me where we were going, yet he had no possible way
of knowing. Right through his Prep and Public School life our
letters crossed in the post although we neither wrote regularly nor
exceptionally. It is still so now.

" The Nuns didn't seem to notice anything unusual about him,
and I am not at all sure really that I did. In fact he was very bored
there, but he was bored on and off for a long time. He went to a
Prep school which was all right to start with, till he took his
Common Entrance at ten and a half with flying colours. No school
would take him till he was at least thirteen, no school his father
approved of that is, though I was all for Dartington, so he had a
very difficult three years. The Head was a good man, and was
interested in him, gave him special work and special coaching.
Even so, he was working on his own which is not a good thing. He
was lucky he didn't stop altogether as he so easily could have
through sheer boredom. He liked games and maybe that was why
he got on well with the other boys, who accepted him.

" This business of his being gifted didn't seem to arise. After
all a child is so malleable at that age, such a tremendous responsibility, and you must do all you can to put things in their way. I

did this with books and his bedside reading at six or seven was Shakespeare! I thought this almost indecent! From a book point of view he did not go through a cowboy and adventure period. He was never keen on comics. We discussed what one wanted out of life—peace of mind, success, money or what. I tried to make it possible for him to have stimulus of all kinds.

" He did well at his Public School and did a lot of things. He took twelve 'O' levels when he was thirteen, then later took some 'A' and then some ' S ' and by that time he was able to go to Oxford. But during the whole of his school life he was hardly ever ' extended.' The School did not send to me and say ' here's a gifted boy.' We had discussed what he wanted and he decided he wanted Oxford, and so he went.

" I divorced my first husband and remarried. Helen, my second child is fifteen and a half. There are eight years between the girl and the boy. They are getting closer now, as they were when young, but there was a time when there was no contact between them at all for several years. I didn't expect that she would be gifted, in fact I was strongly aware that she was very timid and afraid of many things. It drew my attention to myself rather than her. I knew I had a strong personality, but was I overpowering? I had got to make her feel strength in herself, and not to look to me for it. Oddly enough she liked patting ponies over the fences at the age of about two, so when she was four I taught her to ride. It took about six weeks. No school would take her, but because of her liking for horses, which she still has, she got a physical confidence in herself, and from this she became more confident in other ways. She did not walk till nearly two or talk till two or two and a half, but once she started she never stopped. She talked in sentences— and long ones. An incredible vocabulary, and like her brother, questions all the time! I taught her to read at about three and a half and a year later she could read anything, and she wanted to! At school she was considered bright, but because of my husband's job we moved several times and she had to change.

" I chose her present school because, owing to family circum- stances she *had* to go away from home. I knew she had a mind but I was more concerned with the development of her body and of

33

2

her confidence, so I looked for a 'homey' boarding school, and I found one. She was happy there, but she did no work. She went when she was nine and eighteen months later I had a great collection of beautifully drawn horses which she sent me. I thought this remarkable as they had only an hour for letter writing every so often and I asked her how she found time to draw all these horses. She said 'I do it in all the classes. There is nothing else to do.' So I went to the School, and very much against the old-fashioned Head had the girl jumped a year. She got on perfectly well a year in front! In fact, she got on much better and took two 'O' levels at thirteen and six at fourteen with, she told me, only working the year that she jumped. She says now, at fifteen and a half, that she has never done any work since, so I have decided to change schools and send her where there are opportunities for gifted children.

"I've no idea what she wants to do with her life. She's been through phases but hasn't settled yet. I think she will probably finish by writing for the B.B.C. or something like that. She loves words, and all about them. She is more scholarly and academic than her brother. He is more outgoing but she is not an introvert. Most of her friends are about a year older than she is. In the holidays she enjoys anything and everything . . ."

Patricia's own high intelligence is obvious from her detailed account of her two remarkable children's gifts and this is one more case to substantiate the already general belief that such gifts are, to some extent, inherited. The belief is a firm one and probably originated in England. It was in 1869 that Francis Galton the scientific philosopher published his book *Hereditary Genius* and amongst his findings was that first-degree relations of eminent men (brothers, sons, fathers) were in the main of high intelligence. His discovery was based on an investigation into such families, and the number of gifted members of these various families was too high to be put down to chance. Carrying the investigation further he discovered that by the fourth generation there was a marked falling off of gifts and his conclusion was that high intelligence, as an inherited characteristic, ultimately becomes attenuated over the years as a result of the introduction of less intelligent strains.

" Like father like son " is a tremendous generalization but there is a lot in this half-truth although modern knowledge of genetics and environmental factors creates the need to modify such a statement. Modern psychological thought favours a " break-down " of general characteristics into much smaller and easily-defined concepts such as perception of relationships (knowing that a three-inch cube cannot fit into a two-inch hole). A number of such abilities is known as the " G " factor and the special abilities comprising this factor, likewise abilities indicating unusual gifts (music, and the other arts) are testable in their own right. After all, if Galton's theories remained unchallenged and one were to believe that intelligence is purely an inherited factor it might be felt that there would be very little point in providing opportunities for higher education for the children of certain races (or even of certain social groups within these races) as they would not be expected to throw up enough children of high intelligence to make it worth while. At present, however, our knowledge of the factors governing intelligence is incomplete and the only thing of which we can be certain is that both genetic and environmental factors are involved.

There seems to be a slight correlation between general physical development and intelligence. In a recent survey it was found that on the average, middle-class children were taller than working-class children, but working-class children who were selected for Grammar School education were found to be taller than middle-class children who had not been selected and definitely taller than those children from their own social class who had failed to be selected. But perhaps this correlation should be modified, bearing in mind that the comparatively few working-class children who go to Grammar Schools come mainly from homes of skilled workers such as charge hands or foremen, and that until recently low pay and ignorance of the best kinds of food for health will have had an effect on the growth of a child whose father was unskilled.

From the study of certain families, it can be seen that, just as haemophilia can be inherited due to a sex-linked gene, or colour blindness inherited due to alternate genes at a single locus, intelligence in all its aspects appears to persist from one generation to another, although the aspect revealed varies from person to person, the result perhaps of environmental factors. Henry the Seventh was a brilliant administrator and re-organized the country after the Wars of the Roses, encouraged and made possible the revival of learning, and passed on his gifts to his son, Henry the Eighth who, for all his notoriety as a husband, was an outstanding athlete, musician and scholar. Three of *his* children were brilliant—Mary Tudor who worked under Erasmus, Elizabeth the First, also a great ruler, an astute business woman, a lover of the arts and of the highest social intelligence, and Edward the Sixth, whose outstanding scholastic career was cut short by his early death from tuberculosis.

A love of learning, high social intelligence, strong awareness of others and special aptitudes are all strikingly evinced in the following statement by a gifted mother. It will be seen that she is, indeed, especially gifted with awareness, that most necessary quality for the true assessment of a child's gifts and potentialities.

" Deirdre was a very small baby and had to have oxygen. She developed slowly, didn't speak or walk, and slept badly until she was two when we went to Italy for four months. There she began to speak for the first time, *and in Italian*! Suddenly she shot ahead, and when we returned to England, began to speak English. I never had to talk down to her, she was always a good companion and asked questions the whole time. She still wasn't walking, then one day my old Nannie came to see us, put the child on her feet and gave her a little push. Deirdre walked!

" She was very small when she first began to be interested in music. We were living in a flat—she was only three—and the piano was in the hall through which everyone had to pass. One day we found her picking out, with her fists, the notes of ' The First Noel ' which she had heard a few days before. The notes were all correct. Six months later she started piano lessons with a Royal College Teacher who had to be persuaded as she thought the child was too young, but after a quarter of an hour said ' I would like to teach her.' This she did for three years, and Deirdre loved her lessons and her practising.

" When she was four, she taught herself to read, and read well from the first. At five she went to a Montessori school and I think she was bored after a while, but I had great difficulty in finding a school where they wouldn't put her into the kindergarten. Anyway she was always top of her form in spite of having time off for music lessons, so we found an old Frenchwoman who came along and taught her French. This helped to mop up her superfluous energy—she outgrew the school and found the work too easy.

" She went to Kathleen Long for music when she was eight and the year after I persuaded the Reverend Mother at a Convent to take her a year early. There she was with children aged between ten and twelve, was top again except in mathematics, very happy and interested in everything. At this time there simply wasn't a school where musical children could go to in England, where they could have lessons and practise and get a good education at the same time. This was what she really needed, so my husband took her to Paris and Jacques Fevrier heard her play and took her on as a private pupil. On her twelfth birthday she left home and went to live in Paris, and a year later she entered the Conservatoire where she is still.

"At home, Deirdre likes to talk—*all* the family love to talk. They talk all the time, through each other and together. She is interested in philosophical questions and will argue endlessly with my husband and her brothers and sisters. We are Catholics and she has her doubts and difficulties, but these are discussed openly. It is permanently under discussion with us, the Ins and Outs of it all . . . She is growing up now, and recently she fell in love with a man of thirty. It wasn't just the ordinary ' pash ' of a schoolgirl but seemed to be real love and she suffered a great deal. Her pain seemed to colour all her life, her work and her letters, but it has simmered down at last, and she seems to have been able to make a friend of this man and his wife. Boys of her own age bore her, and she seems to frighten them. She is lonely in the way so many gifted children are lonely . . ."

The mothers of Helen and Peter, and of Deirdre come from a certain class, and it is relevant at this point to remember that a few years ago the Crowther Report indicated that the child of an unskilled worker had only a one in a hundred chance of higher education. Undoubtedly our whole attitude to education is coloured by class distinction, and it would seem that many working-class parents of gifted children are as much in need of help as the children themselves, and sometimes more so, especially in the field of School selection.

Very often, such parents do not know which is the better of two Primary Schools to which their child could go, and it is a matter for reflection when we ask ourselves the question: " If Helen and Peter and Deirdre had not been born to parents with educational advantages, would they have been recognized for their worth?" Or does one need to inherit class as well as high intelligence to be assured of the full recognition of gifts and to be given the education best suited to develop such gifts to the full?

4

First Person Singular

"I WONDER what I'm going to be like when I grow up," said Greta, and this is a question that she repeatedly asks. True enough, Greta who is fifteen has more reasons than most for wondering what her future will turn out to be like because there is a strain of mental instability in her immediate family. A concern with the future indicates a kind of dissatisfaction with the present and in general it is only after puberty has been reached, other than in an extreme set of circumstances, with its concomitant emotional upheaval, that any form of dissatisfaction with the present manifests itself. But gifted children are never satisfied either with themselves or their condition, and their everlasting questions can never be answered because the answer, in itself, creates a new question. So in her very early 'teens, Greta is doubly concerned with the future, primarily because she is of the age to query everything, and also because of her particular problem.

In the years of their latency, gifted children are enabled to use all their strong sense of reality in a way which, when they are asked their opinions on this or that, suggests almost a kind of complacency. They seem too sensible to be true. There are emotional difficulties, but at this age, they tend only to emerge in the form of symbolism and fantasy. "You get sections of the community having their own particular ideas about things and if you choose sane or sensible men to represent you, I mean they're not going to have extreme views, except in a few things, so generally they'll be sensible," said thirteen years old Laurence, sitting relaxed in his chair with an air of worldly wisdom which sat on his young shoulders without the slightest effect of self-consciousness. If he has reached puberty, the *sturm und drang* period seems to have

39

done little more than sharpened his awareness of himself into a form of independence, and already he is looking forward to leaving home, but under the friendliest of circumstances. Perhaps he is ridding himself at this time of all the desperate self questionings of all the knowledge that he has so far acquired through his schooling or from his working-class parents. " My children should be brought up to have completely open minds on everything and to believe what they like. I have difficulty in believing in God myself. I would like to believe in God, but really I'd rather not have to think about the matter at all," he continued, and settled back for another un-emotional discussion of almost anything we would have cared to suggest.

" I know what I'm going to be like for the next few years," said fourteen years old Mark, " I shall be at school so my future is assured," and who would have lacked the heart to point out to him that nobody's future is assured. But it was obviously important for him to feel so assured.

So rational and intelligent an attitude augurs well for the problematical future that must be the lot of all of us and it is such a boy who, in times of stress, will be able to come to terms with the sometimes almost overwhelming emotional reactions of early adolescence.

Frank, too, had this unequivocal attitude to profound considera-tions—" it doesn't really worry me (religion) because whether there is a God or not I can't believe that it is going to make any difference to my existence. I don't think that God is so necessary in my world."

These highly intelligent boys, since the time they were able to speak, have been acquiring knowledge in an encyclopaedic fashion but not necessarily applying it to themselves because, as yet, they are not of the years to be able to do so. There is this precociousness which is, nevertheless, part of their charm and shows none of the self-doubt which will one day begin to assail them, when they begin to apply what they have heard, or been told, to their own characters. But not so with Greta who, in her interview with the authors, was making statements and questioning them at the same time in a slightly desperate way.

" First of all I would like unilateral disarmament, but it would have to be unilateral to begin with because it would be just Britain. I think Britain should go first then the other countries would follow. I'm not really sure that they would follow, but it wouldn't do Britain any harm, would it? Then there's the colour bar. I don't think this law they're going to pass is good enough because it doesn't seem to make people want to stop being prejudiced. It can't stop discrimination against Negro lodgers, but it's difficult to know what one can do about this. Negroes don't seem to be given the chance to settle down, the Irish managed it and the Jews, but not the Negroes.

" I like foreigners. I don't think anyone should be banned. I mean if you've got a foreigner who turns out to be a brilliant artist, well that's good for the country isn't it? People just don't seem to recognize foreigners as being human like themselves. They seem to treat them as a species apart. I mean even I discriminate in a funny way. I'd want to offer a Negro a seat in a bus and this is discrimination isn't it? It isn't good. I'd like to feel they were the same as everybody else, but then I wouldn't feel it would I? If I offered my seat like I said, this would make me feel good because this would make me feel different from other people, and I suppose I need to feel better than these people. I suppose it's because I'm not sure of myself."

Greta has reached the age when she is relating experience to her own deepest feelings, which have only just started to emerge. She is now beyond the age when it is easy to make and drop friends without any qualms whatsoever and there are questions of loyalty and emotional dependence to be observed. " I can get led easily by other people and this is a problem. My best friend made me watch football last week and it doesn't interest me at all. She thinks I'm some sort of a God and if I say ' let's go to the Tate Gallery ' she'll come like a shot, so I suppose I'm being dutiful by doing something she wants in return. But most places she likes to go so do I—if not football matches!"

The social loneliness of many highly intelligent children comes over very clearly in her next statement. " I'm not lonely when I'm alone, but I can be lonely when I'm with people. I only like people who like me and not everybody likes me. I'd like a complete fool if they liked me, perhaps not as much as I could but more than a clever person who didn't like me," and already she has learned to make her own assessment of those who seem to be different . . . " I've never met a criminal but there's a boy in our school who pinches things and does stupid things like eating paper. I suppose he's a juvenile delinquent. I don't understand why he has to steal because he comes from a good family. I'm sorry for him but the things he does makes me laugh. I suppose the reason he carries on like this is to draw attention to himself, to be odd because basically he's not bad but needs to appear to be so."

Alan is twelve, a remarkable little boy who is not only one of the most intelligent pupils at his Grammar School (where he is top of his class) but has great sensitivity and warmth which, however, he is unable to demonstrate openly because he is shy and slightly withdrawn. His mother is sweet-natured and easily imposed upon, but his father is far too powerful a character for the good of anyone who cannot stand up to him. As a result, Alan has problems of identification with his father, and a very highly developed sense of protection towards his mother.

Talking about his School, he made a point in a way which we had not encountered before . . . " the teacher in our biology lesson, she tries to put everything too simply and I can't understand a thing. She does everything so simply, says everything so simply, I just can't understand." Obviously Alan's mind has feelers in all directions, and if they are not stimulated his responses become instinctively dulled and he finds he " cannot understand." The reason for under-achievement could not be more graphically and *simply* expressed.

He has the usual problem of the gifted inasmuch as he feels at home with intelligence rather than with age. He feels in no way intimidated by the eighteen years old boys in the Sixth form, but "At school I might like to speak to some boys in the sixth form but they're eighteen and when we are all together eating lunch, I might as well not be there. I asked one of these boys a question once and he just didn't bother to answer."

When asked what sort of girl he would like to marry, this twelve years old boy had some astonishingly rational ideas . . . " I'd like my wife to be interested in the same things as me otherwise what would we talk about? I don't mind if she goes out to work, but only if it's necessary, if we are hard up, otherwise I don't think it's necessary. But I won't be that hard up. I'm bound to get a reasonable salary because if you come from a Grammar School with the advantages of a Grammar School you usually can get a good job with quite a good salary."

Because he is an unusually sensitive little boy, Alan depends more on heart than on brain when he looks for friends. " Once you like a person you can't really tell why you like them. I wouldn't like somebody who didn't have any brains, he would have to be intelligent, but I don't look for intelligent people though I seem to find them, but if I find I can't talk to somebody, this is usually a grown up person, an old person."

On the question of race: " The man and his wife who live next door to me are coloured and I like them very much. He is very friendly, but I think that this is because he hasn't got any children. I wouldn't like to live in a place where there are a lot of coloured people. I would feel that I'm different to them, there are about five or six in our street and that's all right, but if there were more I'd feel that no matter what I thought or what I could do, they'd still be different from me."

Finally the subject of religion, on which Alan seemed to share the undisturbed atheism of so many of the youngsters that were interviewed. " I don't really think there can be a God. There might be something like a force. When the Old Testament and the New Testament were written, people didn't know certain things and facts to do with space, and that certain forces could happen that, to them, might seem like the coming of the Messiah. When Moses went to collect the Ten Commandments there was supposed to be smoke and thunder at the top of the mountain but this might have been a volcano, this is nature, they might not have understood in those days." This is a twelve years old boy's refusal to take an authoritarian explanation on trust and an attempt to satisfy his own reason within the limits of his experience.

Clear thinking, freedom from second-rate opinions and a remarkable freedom, too, from the polite formalities that hidebound parents try to impose upon their children are some of the hallmarks of the gifted child. Helen, aged thirteen, is remarkably self-contained and for all the fact that she only has one good (and musical) friend, can say of her, " She is not much use, she has to practise at weekends." Helen seems to be an opposite from the dreamy Alan (who will spend hours browsing over books, or lying in bed considering all that has occurred during the day) . . . " I like to do things, in fact the worst thing for me is to have to write about things we have done and the next worst is to have to listen to what we are going to do, but the best of all is to do things —experiments are one better than talking " said Helen firmly.

Gifted children are able to use a neat, yet graphic phraseology to express their ideas, even when they are very young, though the things which they may be concerned with are, as yet, normal to others of their own age. " The doll will be one tomorrow. My sister will be eight. She is seven years older than the doll " said six years old Christine categorically, having been asked how old her sister's doll was! Sister Dorothy was, in fact, to be eight the following week, and when we asked whether she was looking forward to the party, Christine replied comprehensively " Yes, there will be a cake with eight candles on it, mummy will make cakes, jellies, trifles—raspberry, strawberry and pineapple jellies—I like best the cake and the drinks. We shall have some orange drinks. There will be ten of us. All but one are girls. Besides having tea, we shall play games, hide and seek, blind man's buff, postman's knock. I like best playing ' be discreet '."

Gavin, with the healthy enjoyment of any eleven years old in model cars and aeroplanes, told us also of his great interest in " the National Society for Prevention of Road Accidents and all its work " (his own words!) and as he lives in a remarkably traffic-free country town, there would seem to be no obvious external reason for the interest. He likes music and rope climbing " but I only venture up about six feet at a time. It is pretty frightening to get off the floor that far." The interests may be usual, but the method of communication is outstanding.

Towards the end of their adolescence, the gifted, having had a certain experience of life, often show a surprising degree of wisdom and intuition in matters of major importance in their lives. They may fall passionately in love and suffer all the anguish but they, unlike the fools, do not rush in where angels fear to tread—" I did not have a boy friend at School because really I was working too hard all the time " said Anne. " When I came to College I went mad and had a succession of them. I have now a steady one. It's serious on his part, but I don't know. He is a Canadian and is not like the usual run of people. He came to England partly because he was tired of everything at home, and he was doing things not because he wanted to, but because everyone else was."

Lastly, there was sixteen years old Malcolm who said that he would much rather write to us than speak to us, and so we let him . . . (though once again there is this slant towards atheism, out of a hundred children to whom we sent a questionnaire those with strong religious beliefs were equal in number to those expressing atheism or agnosticism).

" I don't believe in God. In order not to believe in God it is necessary to believe in something else : if not in after life, then in the value of one's present life, and to do that one must be some sort of an idealist :—all very logical, but it doesn't follow that I am an idealist. It merely shows that I am more easily satisfied than most and that I am reasonable enough in my demands on life never to be radically disappointed. It would be very difficult, at the moment, to make me unhappy for any length of time, because I am still young enough to have a firm belief in life, art, and my own abilities. With this force of optimism behind me, and an un-religious upbringing, I have had no use for the supporting stays of the Church. Religion demands so much for what it gives. Nowadays it makes one, if not ridiculed by, at least estranged from half the population.

" I find myself, like everyone should, of such infinite variety that I have no need to be constantly with other people. That would be to the detriment of my self-knowledge. However, when I am with friends, and enjoying myself, this means that I enjoy myself much more fully than people who are never alone and I miss people, through habit of being alone, much less than would another person who was not used to being alone. Altogether it seems to me that I have got the best of both worlds.

" I am like every adolescent in the world in that I think my potentialities are greater than anyone elses. Sometimes I think that if it were possible for anyone to understand my motives completely, and to know all my thoughts, they would be lost in admiration! As this is an impossibility, my self-worship is secure!

" I have an advantage over many people in having, on the face of it, lived up to a certain amount of self-esteem and in being able to summon frankness and a confidential manner to my aid while simulating the most blatantly false modesty. True humility is known only to a few, and, in the words of ' The Wife of Bath ': ' And Lordings, by your leave, *that* am not I.' Occasionally, by going injudiciously far into my motives for an action, I get humbled by perceiving unjustifiable motives beneath the good ones I had imagined to be the only ones.

" Human motivation—what a maze of fruitless enquiry that yields me nothing but uncertainty. It spreads like the branches and roots of a tree from the action—the trunk. For each action there are two possible motives, a good and a bad. The good motive branches and forks in a myriad of sub-motives up into the free air, and one may follow its twisting and turning to the tiniest twig and still find a motive for *that*. The bad descends from the other end of the action, and one does not care to go beneath the earth beyond the roots' first forks until time strikes down the tree and the good is brought to earth, and the twisted, pale sinews of the bad are brought to light.

" My brother and I were walking down the High Street one day towards his car, when we noticed two girls following us, giggling. They looked about thirteen at the most, were dirty, and each seemed the grotesquely deformed image of a grown-up woman. My brother turned round and asked them if they wanted a lift. They said yes, and they joined us.

" The radiator of the car started leaking, so we drove carefully to our garage and left the car there, walking back over the Heath. It was five thirty, and being winter, it was dark. My brother took the better of the two girls, if better there could be of those two, and made it pretty obvious that he expected me to take the other one. I found I couldn't. Some strong feeling, I did not define it to myself at the time, inhibited me. Eventually we reached the bottom of our road, and as my brother was going past it, I turned towards home. 'Where are you going? ' he asked. 'Home,' I said, walking away. When I got home I felt a compulsive need to rid myself of the incident, and, having no other way, I literally cleansed myself of it : I had a bath. Then I worked out why I had not done what my brother had wanted me to. I put it down to natural disgust, and my belief that my brother had better things to do with his time than this most contemptible form of petty, low pleasure. My refusal became partly one of honour, and partly one of natural superiority, a perfectly excusable form of disgust.

"That evening when my brother came in I admonished him— YES, I ADMONISHED HIM. I needed to, for the same reason that I had needed to have a bath and cleanse myself : to get rid of the other motives which grew the other way out of my part in the incident, and which, if excusable, were ugly and, I sensed, when followed further would become not even excusable. These were resentment at the way my brother treated me as naturally being satisfied with the second best girl, and jealousy at the fact that he had picked them up, not me. These united in a definite wish to spoil his fun. And what had in fact held me back, though it had in part been disgust and superiority (not snobbery) con-sisted mainly of fear. An overwhelming fear of what I did not know and doubt of my own sufficiency and in particular, terror of that inane, empty, idiotic girl's derision. THAT I would not expose my vulnerable superiority to."

5

All the Colours of the Rainbow

―――

"HEAVEN lies about us in our infancy," wrote Wordsworth, but so too does Hell! There is the tangibility of the world around us, the world we can comprehend, but also our own inner and private world peopled not only by the Wise and Kindly Ones who never fail us because they never walked upon this earth, but also by ghosts and dragons so frightening that we have to push them out of sight, where we wish they would remain.

These creatures of darkness and light are our fantasies and they have the power to emerge in forms which arouse overwhelming horror and disgust, but can also give us that glimpse of Wordsworthian heaven.

Both the dark and the light are integral parts of ourselves and until we can reconcile the two sides of our nature, we cannot hope to grow up in a world which cannot accept us until we have achieved this, and thus know ourselves. But this is something we have to learn.

Before we come to terms with reality or, in other words, when we are still children, fact and fantasy, the outer world and our inner world, the animate and the inanimate, are one. Life indeed has all the colours of the rainbow. Fantasy lies at the very root of our existence and its dynamic presence (dynamic because it is unconscious and not open to the modifications of conscious reasoning) accounts for much that we consciously become. Even when we apply adult measures of self-discipline to traits in ourselves which we may dislike, the result of this discipline does not eliminate the unconscious drives resulting in the behaviour felt necessary by us to be modified in the first instance.

48

Sometimes, in our infancy, we have to create our own heaven around us. Asked to write a " composition," Rosemary, a gifted child aged seven, had this to say:

" I think of my family mostly when I think about people.

"A nice sort of family would be a mother and father and a brother and sister.

" My cousins are five children but it seems a much larger family. They live in a block of flats that seem all higgledy-piggledy. They know their way about but to me it seems very large.

" It makes it seem more like a family where there is a baby. All the older children can help look after it. Babies do funny things like getting egg on their nose when they are eating.

" Mothers look after families while fathers go out to work.

" My friends across the road have got two guinea-pigs in their family. We have got Gilli who is a dog. Once we presumed that Gilli was in the car when we were coming back from Leatherhead. When we got home we realized that she wasn't with us. Mummy rushed back next morning and found her in the exact spot where we had left her. Most animals don't live in families. Mother dogs look after their babies but the father dog doesn't because he doesn't breast feed them.

" Human beings need families. Young wild animals can usually go off and find their own food very early and animals who aren't wild just get fed by the people who own them. Children can't go off as soon as they are born. They can't keep their balance and they need to know and be able to do much more than animals. Families teach all kinds of things. I learn all sorts of little things like map reading when we go on journeys and changing my little sister's nappies. Families are nice . . ."

The truth of the matter is somewhat different. Rosemary's father has been married twice and there are two sons by a former marriage and four children by the second, and she obviously feels that the ideal family only has two children in it and, what's more, she to be the only girl! She projects on to her cousins the " higgledy-piggledy " feelings of her own confusion.

This is a moving cry from a little girl who feels swamped by her two-tiered family, and there is the suggestion of regression in a wistful longing for the breast: " Children can't go off as soon as they are born, they can't keep their balance."

To compensate for her confusion at the particular reality around her, Rosemary has to invent the ideal family. All being well, she will come to terms with what she longs for and what she can have, but it is quite likely that when she grows up Rosemary's own family will certainly not have more than two children in it! We are, in fact, in most ways the result of what we were.

The expression " I wish I was young again but knowing what I know today!" is an appeal for the impossible, but if it *were* possible, if we could turn back the clock once again to experience those times when everything seemed to have all the colours of the rainbow, *and* be able to exploit this richness to its best advantage in an adult way, well this would be heaven on earth. Unfortunately it is the very unchecked dynamism of our early fantasies which makes them a potent force in shaping our lives. We are what we are whether we like it or not.

However as a result of our (comparatively new) knowledge of this potency of infantile fantasy, it is possible for enlightened parents to be aware of the quality of their children's imagination and create a climate in which their inner lives and sensibilities will achieve a full flowering. If the child is gifted, the flowers will smell all the sweeter or, to return to our original simile, the colours of the rainbow will be all the brighter.

Gifted children's fantasy life is not basically different from that of the average child, but their ability to express themselves makes recognition of their potential gifts all the easier. An outstanding example of the ability of the gifted child to deploy fantasy in getting under the skin of situations is seen in the following :

The Guy

Here I sit on the bonfire high,
while the rockets are whizzing by,
lots of children having fun,
with fireworks that bang just like a gun.

Sparklers sparkling in the night,
while the flames leap up to a great height,
while I slowly burn down and down,
I hear the fireworks in the town.

In the morning when you wake,
there will be no mistake,
You just wait and you will see,
just dust and ashes I will be.

This was written by eight years old Susan who is a very clever, lively and happy little girl from a good home. Yet the imagery in this poem, written no doubt straight out of mood, is a startling revelation of the awareness of pain and unrequitement—being reduced to dust and ashes while everyone else is having fun. Susan also wrote the following :

Cockle-Bockle

Once upon a time there lived a little elf named Cockle-Bockle. He was so small and delicate that he was quite invisible to see to the human eye. Cockle-Bockle lived in a big house. Now, in that same house there also lived a girl named Mary. One day Mary was looking about when she saw a speck lying on the ground. So she went to get her magnifying glass. She looked at it closely and there lay Cockle-Bockle asleep.

Mary was quite astonished and Cockle-Bockle was even more. The girl picked up Cockle-Bockle and put him in a jar, where she left him with only a few holes in the top for air. Poor Cockle-Bockle, there was no way of escaping. Then, suddenly, Cockle-Bockle had an idea. He would push and push so he could get the lid off, it was only resting on the top. At last it came off, but how was he to get out of the glass for it was very slippery.

Then Cockle-Bockle had another idea. Some mistletoe berries had fallen into his jar, so he stuck them on to the side to make steps. So Cockle-Bockle climbed up the side and jumped down. At last he was free again. He wandered over the window sill and then suddenly fell plop over the window sill into the sink.

There was some water in the sink, but suddenly the plug was pulled out. He tumbled down the drain pipe and landed with a bump on the ground. He wandered about in the tall grass and oh! he was swallowed by an adder. So Cockle-Bockle climbed up his bones and jumped out. He again wandered about in the grass till he came to a large farm. He walked about till he came to a pail of milk : he climbed up the side to see what was in it. But oh dear he fell in. The maid came and took the pail of milk to milk the cow.

Now it happened that Cockle-Bockle was having a nice look around when he was swallowed by the cow. The cow coughed and spluttered and Cockle-Bockle fell out, he wandered on to fairy land, he got there and stayed for ever.

If we did not know that the youthful author was a contented child we would be overwhelmed by the pathos of this essay in despair and want to rush out and comfort her before, indeed, she escaped from the world of reality and went into fairy-land forever. Small and delicate—invisible to the human eye—a speck lying on the ground. What could be plainer than this description of feeling unimportant, unloved and overlooked? The idea of using mistletoe berries as steps to get out of the jar is also a stroke of imaginative genius. Don't we kiss under the mistletoe? Isn't it to do with love? So love was necessary in order to escape from slipping into the vortex, yet love too had to be trampled on in order to escape. Susan's gift of empathy and her ability to conjure up striking imagery and, above all, her facility in the use of strongly emotive words already gives an indication of a talent for imaginative writing which may well develop into substantial achievement if she makes it her aim.

Andrew aged eight and a half recently changed his address— in fantasy! When one reads his lively and beautifully written piece " Horror House " it is obvious that Andrew has come to terms with many of his own personal ghosts (the boy in the story thought the skeleton was lovely) and it is the father who, in the end, is driven out, taking his family with him.

" It was 1763 and the old house was silent when a scream rang out. AAAH! And then it came EEEEH! The butler ran to his master's room and what he saw made him gulp. There on the floor was his master's body with no head!

The caretaker completed the story.
" And the old 'ouse 'as been 'aunted ever since."
" Now," said Mr. Banks, " let's go in."

(Then follows a frightening description of unexplained noises and events...)

. . . " the bedroom door opened and a bloodstained hand crawled in and on to the bed . . . he looked around seeing chains, bells, model feet, arms, heads, a tape recorder (sic!) and red, green, blue, yellow and orange lights . . ."

Skeletons walk out of cupboards, articles disappear, ghosts fly all over the place and in the end the house wins, the father buys a new one leaving the present house to the ghosts and . . .

. . . " the Banks family packed and left the house. They now live in a house with no spooks . . ."

The use of symbolism in childish fantasy, the reason sometimes for the very positive impact of the writings of the very young and gifted, springs paradoxically enough from a negative source, the inability to face the fears and hatreds that arise in their own breasts towards those they truly love. It is well known that the mother who is loved for what she gives, is hated for what she denies, but unable to face this awareness of the hatred the child has to translate such feelings into symbols sufficiently removed from reality not to be recognized for what they really stand for. It is a form of childish self-deception. This is the reason for the universality of fairy stories, the heroes and princes who overcome dragons, and witches or ghosts intent on destruction.

Nothing is black and white although the child cannot appreciate this, and the more gifted and sensitive the child the more he will be confused by his need for a continually changing assessment of what he believes his parents (or parent substitutes) to be.

Projection, too, is an expression of fantasy when the reality is too painful to be faced. Carl Jung had a very difficult relationship with his father while his mother was kindness personified. Nevertheless, recalling his childhood, he remembers what he felt at the time :

" I am restless, feverish, unable to sleep. My father carries me in his arms, paces up and down singing his old student songs . . .

to this day I can remember my father's voice singing and the still-
ness of the night. I was suffering, my mother told me afterwards,
from general eczema. Dim intimations of trouble in my parents'
marriage hovered around me. My illness in 1878 must have been
connected with the separation of my parents. My mother spent
several months in a hospital in Basle and presumably the illness
had something to do with the difficulties of the marriage . . . I
was deeply troubled by my mother's being away. From then on I
always felt mistrustful when the word " love " was spoken. The
feeling I associated with " woman " was for a long time that of
innate unreliability. " Father " on the other hand meant reliability.
That was the handicap that I started off with. Later these early
impressions were revised. I have trusted men friends and been disappointed by them, and I have mistrusted women and I was not
disappointed."

In the fantasy writings of gifted children we are privileged to
have access to the childish mind in a way no other method could
achieve :

> " The camel is very funny,
>   just look at the size of his tummy,
>   he has two humps on his back,
>   he hates to feel a whack,
>   especially on his back,
>   his humps look heavy to me,
>   and he never goes out to tea."

wrote another young Andrew who seems to know quite a lot about
the anatomy of camels, but the last line seems quite removed from
the rest of the little poem which is undeniably realistic. This
sudden jump into fantasy could easly have come out of mood. Maybe he was feeling slightly lonely at the time and was longing to be
asked, or taken out to tea!

What sort of problem is Carol (aged ten) experiencing, as manifested in her poem " The three beasts of the North Wind " by a
series of questions.

> " Three days ago tomorrow,
>   I saw a treacle bird,
>   I asked him where the North Wind blew,
>   but I never heard a word.

Three days ago tomorrow,
I saw a hefelumpe,
I asked him where the North Wind blew,
but all I heard was ' Grump!'

Three days ago tomorrow,
I saw a striped tangerine,
I asked him where the North Wind blew,
but all he did was grin.

Three days ago tomorrow,
I saw three ugly things,
They told me where the North Wind blew,
and sent me there on wings."

Life must seem full of problems to a gifted and sensitive ten years old, but it is interesting to note that the questions, when asked of such attractive symbols as a treacle bird, a " hefelumpe " and a striped tangerine could not be answered. It needed, alas, " three ugly things " to show the way to that which contained the answer—the North Wind.

There is above all joy to be had in fantasy for fantasy's sake: (The Author is eight years old.)

Animals

" The scientists study the hippo.
(the smallest thing ever born.)
It eats pickled onions and teacups,
and it lives in an underground lawn.

The worm is as large as a house,
with prickles all over its back.
It laughs and giggles all over the place,
and it also says ' Clackity Clack.'

A popular dish is snapdragon,
who flits about the flowers.
It eats sawdust and cream and insects,
and lives inside the towers.

The quail is a beautiful fish,
it lives in the Gangebong.
It eats boiled eggs on toast,
and thumps all day on a gong.

The poach makes elephants cross,
it tickles their nose so they sneeze,
and he lays his skin away all night,
with ' Return if lost, if you please.'

The little birds have bright blue bills,
and on their heads they stand,
so rock yourself my children,
to this place called Wonderland . . ."

There is a reversal of roles in the following poem, for it is an onion which is crying rather than causing others to cry :

The Sad Onion

" An onion sat crying,
upon a big dish,
when he saw the steak frying,
he wanted to wish
his turn would not come,
like the steak to be done."

But it's no good wishing. What will be will be !

" An onion lay bare,
in a polythene bag,
which had an enormous tear,
so he started to sag,
but escape was not near,
for he was pickled that year."

The young (eight years old) author of this poem would seem already to have an unusual acceptance of life's vicissitudes !

In later days many gifted people damaged, perhaps, by lack of recognition when they were young, continue to live a life of fantasy and everyone knows of the novelist who does not write or the painter who does not paint, and not only would it be uncharitable to lump them altogether as inadequate people who cannot face their inadequacies, but it would be untrue. Certainly, for whatever reasons, they have opted out of the struggle and it is especially heartening, therefore, to meet someone very young whose fantasies soar to the heavens but whose sense of reality is such that already, at the age of six (see next chapter), he has constructed an ingenious tree house. Fortunately he is not satisfied with the limitations that reality imposes on him and this will always be a spur to make ever greater efforts in order to attempt the unattainable. At the moment he compensates in a dreamy contemplation of what the tree house might develop into:

" We might get some steel girders and build a look-out tower on top of our hut where we can see the stars and the rooftops for miles around. It will be so high that it will be taller than the trees and taller than the school. We might even put planks across to the bedroom windows and make a passageway to the school. And in Summer when it is very hot we will take out the corrugated iron and push it a little way under the roof so that it sticks out so that we can sit in the shade. We will go on making the hut for a long time—until the end of the term and even next term. We will go on with it until we leave school and then we will give it to our younger brothers and sisters, if our mothers have more babies they will come to this school and it will still be there."

Outstanding in this account for so young a child is the sense of continuing time. " Until the end of term and even next term " and the fact that he wants to leave the housetree that he has built and values, for the rest of his family and even for the unborn babies that their mothers might have. This sense of building something of permanent use to others is seldom seen or so clearly expressed in so young a child.

Finally here is a *cri du coeur* from eight years old Judith who, in a delightful list of amenities she hopes to enjoy when she is grown up, makes it all so plain what she longs for nowadays (travel by boat, the right size of satchel, the ability to go back into history) and also what she *thinks* she ought to have gleaned, no doubt, from listening to adult conversation (visual telephones, Paris fashions, etc.) and heightened by fantasy (velvet-lined Hovercraft).

Myself in Twenty Years Time

" My name is Mrs. Johnson. I am a doctor at Great Ormond Street hospital for children. I have three children all girls. But two are twins.

My husband is a plastic surgeon at the same hospital. We live in a large house.

In our lounge I have a lovely rocking chair that can be made into a bed which is comfortable. We also have a colour television which the children detest when cowboy films are on. The television is portable and is ideal when someone is ill.

The children have a study where there are three adding machines and typewriters. The schools have heated indoor swimming pools and covered playing fields. Last week the outing was to Norway and I think that this week's is to Fiji Islands. Their geography is outstanding and I'm sure they know more than me.

My lucurys (sic) are a teamaker and a telephone which you can see the people you are talking too.

We girls wear a short light dress in Summer and fur boots, gloves and a long dress in Winter. The men wear long trousers and a wooly furry jumper in Winter and short tunics in black or blue in Summer. Satchels are never heavy or too small and work is easy and quick to do. My children go to school on a boat which can take up to 100 children.

Trains are much larger with games room and television on it. Every train has a dining room. Buses are no longer but a hovercraft is in use. This one in our town is lined with velvet and is very comfortable. A hovercraft took me to shop in Paris and I bought a lot of Paris fashions and enjoyable food which we had for tea. Rockets are beginning to take passengers anywhere. I have a new N.F. car which is useful. In the back is a little table and a cupboard where I keep food and drink. A telephone and television are there as well. Long journeys go too quickly because of this. I like going to golf because instead of a caddy we have a car to play from.

Our Summer house is in New Zealand near Dunedin. It is sometimes so hot we have to go home in case we get sunstroke. But every weekend we go to Dunedin. The river are lovely to swim in. Then after a swim we have a portable heater which helps to dry quickly. Time machines are being invented and I hope to live long enough to see the Vikings by the time machine.

This is how I hope to be in twenty years time."

6

A World of Their Own

===

"**MR. SALTEENA** was an elderly man of 42 and was fond of asking peaple to stay with him." Thus runs the opening sentence of a famous novel and in its mis-spelling of the word *people* we get the first of a series of glorious literary felicities and a slight clue (*elderly* man of 42!) that the author was not—well, exactly mature in years. She wasn't. Daisy Ashford was nine years old when she wrote *The Young Visiters*, a little masterpiece of precocious observation and a book which, one hopes, will never be out of print for very long.

What is so remarkable about *The Young Visiters* is not its cuteness, but its length—It runs to about twenty thousand words—bearing in mind that the authoress had not even achieved two figures in her chronological age. In the field of childhood activities, it is this element of total absorption and the carrying out of projects to an unusual degree of achievement by which one can recognize unusual gifts.

Gifted children, when they indulge in activity, do so with a degree of concentration and a purposefulness which is not all that common in an adult. Not only that, but there is a diversity of interests, all of which are practised, because the age of specialization has not been reached, the time when they know, finally, what they want to achieve most in life, and canalize their energies accordingly.

When we examine the current activities of such children, there is no hundred percent. guarantee that their fecundity and energy will continue into the time when they are able to capitalize on it to some practical end, so it might be as well to select, to begin with, someone whose adult achievement was in every way a flowering of what, in her early days, can be seen to be the concerns of a child of unusual gifts.

Few people will not have heard of Octavia Hill, and they will also be aware of her great and pioneer work in housing and her efforts to protect the English countryside from the ravages of industry and speculative jerry-building, efforts which led directly to the formation of the National Trust.

Octavia Hill was a remarkable woman, and when we probe into her early years we realize that she was a remarkable child. Her energy knew no bounds. She longed for a field " so large that I could run in it forever " and if, for the word " field " we substitute " world " (to so young a child such a field could be the world) then we have a graphic illustration of what it is like to be blessed with a mind that needs space and freedom to indulge in its multifarious facets.

" She can scarcely walk. She goes leaping as though she were a little kangeroo," wrote her mother, and this tremendous core of energy imbued every activity of the remarkable little girl. Octavia was a great letter writer, and their contents, too, reflect the prismatic cast of her mind which detailed and highlighted everything into its most colourful aspects . . . " We have a box full of silks, I gave Miranda a beautiful piece, it was velvet and the colours were black, purple, yellow, white and green. Miranda gave me a beautiful piece of crimson plush." Here one can appreciate the sensual pleasure of a rich nervous system, because of the way such description, so alive to the writer, becomes equally alive to the reader.

It seemed that nothing failed to interest Octavia, and the activities of other people, especially craftsmen, filled her with delight. She pleaded to use the tools of the local carpenter and it is on record that he found her " wonderfully handy " with them. She spent much time gardening, and she adored animals. Octavia loved life, even when she was a little girl, and used her desire for knowledge to further her involvement in life.

This was nearly a hundred and thirty years ago, but gifted children do not change down the centuries. Their liveliness knows no bounds, and they seize on every opportunity to extract whatever they

can out of it and then, by wishing to reveal what they have discovered, put twice as much back. Before the time comes when
they have finally decided what role they will play in life, this extraordinary and undirected fund of energy manifests itself to the
onlooker in a show of such diversity and achievement that one feels
breathless at the continuous display. And it is activity that has a
" professional " touch about the way it is carried out.

Nicky is just sixteen. His brother (aged seventeen) was short
of money. When Nicky's father arrived home one evening he found
an illuminated scroll hanging from a wall bracket on which was
written, in beautifully executed gothic print, and in a suitably
archaic grammatical style, a request from the boy on behalf of his
brother for the loan of one pound! Nicky's bedroom is a revelation
—his own work is everywhere, prints, paintings, cartoons—and it
would be difficult to say, if one did not know, that this was the
work of an untrained artist. There is a day-to-day diary in which
the entries are discourses on such themes as death and marriage,
and the quality of the writing is such that, again, one feels it to be
the work of a professional. There are exercise books scattered
everywhere, full of thoughts, ideas, stories (always complete) and
everything written with an economy of words, yet with a remarkable
power of description, which suggests that already the boy is accomplished in imaginative writing. But what is he to be? Writer? Artist?
Typographer? He is all of them.

When John was nine years old, King George Vth died. All
the children in the small Independant school he attended were
fascinated by the preparations for the State Funeral, but trust
John to think of giving a State funeral to one of the school puppets
that had become too old for further use. The puppet was put in a
box and lay in state in a sand pit. There was a long procession of
mourners, all having been requested to provide themselves with
handkerchiefs and any pieces of black they could find for arm bands,
they walked round the puppet, sniffing and groaning having been
directed by John to " sob loudly," and later came the funeral oration
in which the puppet's great achievements were named one by one.
But even fantasy can have frontiers, and John insisted that such
utter perfection was not lifelike, and the status quo was restored

61

by a final homage to the dead puppet's excellence as a cat burglar! Fired to emulate the radio programme "In Town Tonight," John compèred "visiting personalities," held the microphone at the right angle, and urged the subject not to be nervous and not to shout. He also acted as producer for a school adaptation of the "Wraggle Taggle Gypsies" for which he made an ingenious contraption so that when the time came for "My Lord to ride high and low" the scenery moved and trees and bushes whizzed past in the best back projection manner. Today, not surprisingly, John is a television producer.

That which is dull and repetitive is of no interest to the gifted child, but that which is variable and seems to obey no unquestioned law attracts his attention, and then he wishes to be involved with it. Such an intangible as weather is often on the mind of a clever child—it is always changing and so it captures his interest. Susan, aged nine, is part of the Weather Reporting Team in a South East London School. She is pretty and neat, and her movements are as precise as her thought. Demonstrating a wind gauge to the authors, Susan explained that " it goes round and round and then we look with a stop watch to see how fast it moves. We also use the maximum and minimum thermometers, and the wet and dry ones." Susan regarded her work as fun, and obviously, when she is old enough to work for her living there is no doubt that she will seek out the sort of occupation which she will enjoy. Not for Susan the compromise of learning to like the job you get if you can't get the job you like.

At the moment of writing, a unique experiment is under way at Sevenoaks Public School (Kent) where, under expert guidance, a team of boys who are technologically gifted are being encouraged to use their gifts to their very capacity, the aim being to increase creativity. To visit the Technical Centre at this School is to be awed by the achievement of these remarkably gifted boys, awed not only by the originality of their thought but by the tremendous and sustained efforts involved in directing such thought to practical ends. There is an electronic machine which " plays "—with its operator—the famous old game of not being the last to pick up a match from a collection of matches. In the process, the mind of the boy inventor is pitted against the electronic mind of the very machine he has invented. There is a revolutionary set of traffic signals, again dependent on electronic impulse and, it would appear, more efficient than the signals at present in use on our roads. A boy has invented a machine specially for a cocktail party in order to save the time wasted in spreading pâté onto water biscuits—biscuit and pâté are fed into the machine separately and come out attached to each other! A slightly science-fiction looking engine, not much bigger than a toy train, rattles around a track of white chalk! Electronic impulses, again, were being activated by the chalk line to which the tiny engine keeps as rigidly as if it is being guided by hand. Some of the boys in the Sevenoaks experiment are in their very early 'teens, yet their work entails anything from three months' exclusive concern with the complex things they are trying, and succeeding, to do. It is here that the determination to pursue activity until a degree of perfection is reached—a sign of the truly gifted—can be seen at its most startling.

" I wonder why it looks so big outside and feels so small inside? " asked a boy aged six, gazing reflectively at the tree house he and some contemporaries had constructed, and which was so efficiently and stoutly built that it accommodated four of them, and in this excitingly-placed edifice, they had " feasts " and " made plans." The authors wanted to know how he had built this tree house, and coolly he informed them that it was simply a matter of finding some plants, an iron frame, and splitting a tree trunk in half.

But it looked bigger from the outside. The achievements of the gifted, indeed, are far ahead of their capacity to understand the science behind the action. In the case of some girls at a Primary School, none of them over ten years old, they fashioned musical instruments which they learned to play, and one of them, at least, had a flair for writing drama yet was hopeless at acting for she was nowhere near the age where the mechanics of " projection " could be employed to transport her inside the very characters she had so successfully created. By virtue of their astonishing liveliness of mind, gifted children are, perforce, obliged to put the cart before the horse.

The schism between achievement and the understanding of how, precisely, the achievement is accomplished is in itself yet another stimulus to such children who, as a consequence, become interested in the problems of relationship and growth (" this bit of me fills everybody with delight, but *this* bit of me makes them disappointed. Why? ") and the subjective interest is soon externalized into other fields, according to individual bent, growth in nature (plants, seeds and so on) and a concern with development in general, the process in which one thing becomes another, and the comparison this entails. Mary was so dissatisfied with her worthy but dull Private School that she insisted on leaving to go to a neighbouring Grammar School where she could learn, as she put it, Proper Biology and thus precipitate her journey to the career of her choice, that of a farmer. Mary is nine years old! Frank, a pupil at a South London Primary School, was clutching a plastic bag full of bark when the authors spoke to him. There were, he was anxious to convey, eight different kinds of bark and he had gathered a sample of each that very afternoon because if they are all gathered at the same time they don't dry up unevenly and, therefore, are easier to compare! Frank is eight years old.

The list could be extended, and it is a joy and a privilege to be in the company of these remarkable children, all of them so brimful with vitality, so engrossed in their pursuits, and so delighted to communicate their enthusiasms and their discoveries. They have, at their tender years, found the world to be a fantastic, extraordinary and exciting place, so full of a great many things from cabbages to kings.

Gifted children are inventive at home and at school, love to find new ways of solving old problems, are scornful of stereotyped formulas, preferring to make their own discoveries rather than accept, dutifully, the discoveries of others, use all five of their senses to their greatest advantage, and are capable of throwing new light onto basic problems even at Primary School age. All they ask is that they should be recognized and given the freedom that they need to exercise their undying curiosity.

Sensitive far beyond their years, they can so easily be frustrated in their desire to expand, and the drive of their energy, in extreme

What came first, chicken or egg !

The never-ending curiosity of the gifted child

OIL PAINTING OF KING CHARLES I
ARTIST UNKNOWN
GIVEN BY MR. FRANK BURTON, GREEN DOOR, NEWPORT.

cases, can go inwards and destroy them. So, bearing in mind that their hallmark, rather than the range of their interests, is the determination and skill with which these interests are pursued, it is this element in their activities which needs to be recognized, and once recognition is given them, there is little in the world around them which will not occupy their attention, their investigation and their sympathy.

3

7

Great Expectations

IN a well-loved fairy story, the parents of Prince Prigio offended a wicked fairy by omitting to invite her to their son's christening. In the best tradition of such tales the boy, instead of being the recipient of a blessing, was cursed instead. " My child " said the Wicked Fairy " you shall be too clever " and for many years the poor prince was shunned by all because he knew too much. Finally his wife persuaded him to don a wishing cap, but as one cannot cancel one's own christening and the gift therefore could not be returned he had to be content with the compromise wish of " seeming " to be no cleverer than others.

It is not only in fairy stories, unfortunately, that to be too clever can amount to a curse (as the two case histories in the next chapter prove only too clearly) but here we are concerned with the other side of the coin—failure to live up to parental expectations when one is obviously gifted.

High intelligence does not come from heaven. At least one of the parents of a gifted child is usually also of high intelligence. But high intelligence is not automatically correlated with the kind of humanity which results from insight—the knowledge which allows us to know where we finish and others begin. There is a tendency for many parents of gifted children to project onto them their own hopes and fears and, in the process, attempt to force a child's mind into a shape which it is not suited to become, or impose a mantle of achievement which it is not ready to assume.

This is, occasionally, resented to such an extreme that the child will wilfully play down its own gifts or choose a way of life which is guaranteed to bring disappointment to the parents but, in the process, taking much of the joy out of the child's own life. He has been goaded into a state of rebellion.

Helping anything to grow is an art, whether it be roses or children and so far as gifted children are concerned, America can in one way teach us a valuable lesson. The American quarterly publication *The Gifted Child* throws open its columns to parent, child and teacher alike, all can state their point of view and, as a result, the level of permissive understanding achieved is high. In a recent issue, the gifted mother of a gifted child—she a professional artist and the child talented in the same direction—complained at the boy's apparent inability to accept the limitations of achievement normal to his age (he was only seven). She was unaware that the boy, being head and shoulders above his contemporaries in so many things, felt he ought to be head and shoulders above his mother also, and could not understand his frequent outbursts of hysterical frustration when comparing his efforts with hers. There is no such specific outlet in this country where a delicate state of affairs in an important and effective relationship can be broached, but such a situation is not uncommon to one degree or another.

Parents of gifted children often forget that their sons and daughters are, indeed, *children*, and such a child needs to work out its normal developmental problems not to any lesser extent than the most dim-witted child, but in a considerably more complex way, because the level of complexity and sensitivity of such a mind is that much higher. Above all, they need to be allowed to set their own sights and cover ground at their own speed for, like any child, if forced they will underplay their hand. If it is a good hand, the failure to win the game will seem all the more pronounced.

Elspeth is now aged nine. Her father, just over fifty, has a fairly senior position in one of the " Big Five " banks. The mother is some fifteen years younger, a warm and loving person but not particularly interested in her daughter's scholastic achievements. Oddly enough the pressure in this family comes from the paternal grandmother who is very proud of the family's progress. " One member is a doctor, one went to University and one is in the Bank " she tells everyone, and it was she who saw to it that her granddaughter had "proper" books when she was very young. Actually Elspeth loved her books and by the time she went to Infant School (at five) she could read and comprehend well. Work remained fun until she was seven and started Junior School, and Grannie began to ask how she was doing at school and whether she was top of the form. It was (and is) a particularly good school and the Headmaster realized that Elspeth was gifted. When the child was tested her I.Q. was found to be over 140.

Life should be a delight for such a child, but in a conventional and unimportant spelling test, Elspeth spelt the word "because" as *becase*. When the mistake was pointed out to her she burst into tears and said over and over again in angry despair "I don't make mistakes, I *don't* make mistakes!" Such a cry could only be put down to one thing. The Headmaster saw the father and warned him of the danger of pressure. "You don't know my mother!" replied the man, but he realized that he must stop the devastating pressure that was being applied to Elspeth, took action, and for the first time quelled this over-zealous woman. A recent composition by Elspeth called "On a Wet Day" ended thus : "I enjoyed splashing through the puddles and when I went to bed I thought what a lovely day it had been." This speaks for itself.

When David was seven, his mother found him cuddling their cat late one night. "It's all I've got" he said pathetically "I'm afraid something is going to happen to you." The boy had sensed that his parents were unhappily married, and that his security was threatened. Indeed, two years later, the father left the home.

David's father never liked the boy very much and nowadays, just out of his "teens," it would appear that David is determined to be everything his Jewish father wasn't—devoted to his faith, concerned selflessly with humanity (youth leadership, sociology, membership of the C.N.D.) and, above all, far less overtly accomplished than his high intelligence would seem to demand.

A glimpse of David's background seems to make sense of his underachievement. His father always sneered at his mother's successful attempts to run a business. If David concentrated on exploiting his gifts, wouldn't this mean he would be better than his mother, like his father always had to be? And if he was better than his mother who loved him and brought him up, wouldn't this make him despise her—as his father despised her?

All that David's mother sees is that her brilliant son has utterly failed to exploit his gifts, but she could not be aware of the complex unconscious pattern which, perhaps, is the cause of David's failure. This is an unusual case, and David is now so set in his pattern of life that it is unlikely he will ever recognize his attitude for what it basically is—rebellion against his father—and will continue to fail to rise to the expectations of the one who loves him most because, paradoxically, he loves her in return.

Too few are the parents who can utterly forget their own hopes and fears when it comes to doing what is best for their children. By the natural law of things, it appears so very often that one's child has to contain what is best for the feelings of the parent, and not for the genuine well-being of the child. " This hurts me more than it hurts you " can be meant in more ways than one.

Finally, it is as well if we print in full the statement of faith that was made to the authors by the mother of a gifted spastic child, a statement which should serve as an object lesson in supreme tolerance to all parents whose expectations of their children are disappointed:

" ' You know your child is not only physically handicapped but a mental defective as well,' said a General Practitioner to me over the telephone. But after two years of agonized watching I knew that some intelligence was there, although at three she still had no speech and could not sit up alone. We then moved to Ghana for four years where we had sun and swimming and a relaxed African nannie. There I began talking to Joanna as if her speech were normal, singing, and reading aloud to her. She learned the local language from her nurse and to this as to English she replied with signs and then gradually with a few words and phrases.

" When Joanna was seven we returned to England and there was a disastrous three year period at a school that was experimenting with total immobility in locked calipers, redeemed only by a devoted teacher who taught the children, among other things, to appreciate pictures. Watchful parents became disquieted, a row ensued and Joanna came home to a day spastic unit. This was a single room school with children of all ages and intelligences, but the therapy was first-class and a teacher who was a natural genius got Joanna using her hands on clay, sand, paint and wooden letters. She learned to read fairly fast but by the age of twelve she was barely able to print, in straggling letters about an inch high. Spelling was a great problem; no amount of reading (apparently) teaches one how to spell without the actual practise of writing, and as Joanna began to write she spelt phonetically. At one time I thought this would never be cured but we played word games like Lexicon and her desire to win taught her to spell.

" Meanwhile I had come to a decision. I was obviously going to have to spend a lot of time with Joanna, and Joanna, at some time, would have to spend a lot of time with herself. I would have to try to interest her in all the things I was interested in—music, painting and architecture, literature, religion, languages, partly in self-defence, and partly to give her resources within herself. This had its disadvantages; not only was it not a modern specialist education (what examinations would it teach her to pass?) but it would set her apart from the average of her age group even more than the panic created by her difficult speech. Companionship too was very hard to find. For years her only young friend was my cleaner's child, a year older, strong, affectionate, willing but with no intelligent interests at all. We welcomed and suffered her, because other children who came to tea preferred to talk to *me*!

" Until she became too heavy (when she was about fourteen) I carried Joanna everywhere, over ploughed fields and up Norman castles, even once all round Knole when her wheelchair was refused admittance. I sat beside her for hours answering her questions. Often I could not understand what she said and had to find the key word of a sentence by going through the letters of the alphabet until she stopped me. I got books from libraries, read them at night myself, and passed them on. Joanna was given a wireless which she could use herself. We began to look up programmes in the *Radio Times*. She acquired the habit of marking programmes as soon as a new issue came out. Landmarks stand out—the day when I was able to stop " rationing " music for fear of boring her (she had been listening with me to Berlioz' " Fantastic Symphony ") and at the end said "wonderful, although it's rather a long symphony isn't it?"

"At the age of twelve Joanna went for an interview at the Delarue Grammar School. She could hardly write and spoke very indistinctly so her performance for the first few terms seemed disappointing. Her high intelligence was certainly known to me and the educational psychologist who had tested her, but it seemed like an act of faith as few people had the time or patience to sit spelling out those long queries and answering them. I felt someone might say "parents always overestimate their children's abilities." The great thing with spastics is never to expect too much. Only the knowledge that to expect too little is a drearily diseducating principle to work on kept me optimistic. Meanwhile Joanna was slowly learning to type, although nothing much came of it for two years since, having learned to communicate in laborious print, she was not used to writing more than the bare minimum.

"Suddenly it all began to pour out, first in letters to me in the lively style of her discussions at home, then some time later it infected her essay style at school. Here the long conversations, the reading aloud, the talks about words began to bear fruit in a confident natural style. Still there was doubt about her ability to sit examinations, for she was still getting low marks at school and was fifteen before she could type at a reasonable speed.

"One day she wrote in despair that she had been taken out of the 'O' level class. I collected my wits and wrote pleading that it was worse not being allowed to try than to fail, and that the failure of someone so heavily handicapped could not reflect discredit on the school. She was given a trial run through two papers and did fairly well. Now she has five 'O' levels, is doing two 'A' levels and an extra 'O' in Spanish. Schoolwise, the worst of the fight is over, and recently a cartridge loading tape recorder has cleared up the difficulty of taking notes from classes and books. Now the Ministry is probably giving her an electrically operated chair which will make her mobile at least in large buildings.

"'All this must have been a great strain on you', people say. Yes—and no. It has been an excitement and a privilege to see the steady and modest unfolding of a mind, against all obstacles, the disappearance of frustration as the years passed, the warm appreciation of all one has done. Joanna is growing up into a friend whose company I enjoy. She is lively, interested in a very wide range of things, sociable, competent at organizing her life and a good deal wiser than her parents."

This record of the fight of one intelligent mother of a gifted but tragically handicapped girl shows better than any statistical results of research that gifted children need their parents to believe in them if they are to believe in themselves.

8

Devious Routes

WHEN we are very young, we are taught that the shortest distance between two points is a straight line. But rare indeed is the person who can envisage a successful future and work towards it without deviating from the shortest course. A genius can, sometimes, do this and, in the process, hurt many people. An unscrupulous business man can do likewise, riding roughshod over anything and anybody that stands in his way. Both have an overweening ambition which cannot afford to take account of the human element, either in themselves or in others. But what of a mind of high intelligence that seems to turn against itself in such a way that the owner is not only unable to use it to practical advantage, but is compelled to commit the sort of aggressive acts which can only boomerang back and make him the sufferer? Far from pursuing a straight line, life seems to follow a vicious circle of self-destruction.

It is a popular fallacy that all highly intelligent children can use their intellectual gifts to come to terms with personal problems, and thus make a satisfactory adjustment to life. As we have seen in " inconsequential " children, this is not necessarily so, and many delinquents of high intelligence are around to prove this point. They are, in fact, using their gifts to further their anti-social aims.

Often, however, behaviour which brings a youngster into the clutches of the law amounts to an unrecognized cry for help, a cry which has become distorted through early and intolerable emotional stress, so there is never the possibility of a direct appeal for help, in so many words, from a world which has proved damaging and which is therefore mistrusted. It is like the puppy run over by a

73

bicycle, lying whimpering in the road, and attempting to bite the sympathetic hands that reach down to pick it up and alleviate its pain. The force that injured it, and the hands that wish to help it, are as one.

In many cases, all that is required to help a child or young adolescent who has " gone off the rails " is someone who is not involved in the emotional network surrounding the " victim " and is yet felt to " understand." Even then, the road is a hard and difficult one, because the damage of the years cannot be mended in a matter of weeks or of months. But a beginning can be made, and often a new route through life can be taken, not the way of a straight line, but a devious way which, nevertheless, can lead to a reasonable future. A future, at least, that is not made bleak by the self-destruction of neurotic delinquency.

The highly gifted, although neurotic, delinquent is up against two problems in the uncertain and painful voyage to re-adjustment. He is up against the distorted drive of his own neurosis which should, in the unravelling, be enough for him to contend with, and he is further up against the instinctive awareness of his difference on the intellectual level. Thus, far from being the means to enable him, with help, to return to a more socially acceptable attitude, his intelligence can in itself be yet another difficulty to contend with. Intelligence which is suspect to the owner, because of the isolation it seems to bring by its very possession, is hardly likely to be used willingly to solve personal problems.

Briefly, the boy or girl of high intelligence who seems condemned to a life of trouble, is someone who has grown up physically and intellectually, but not emotionally. The acts of aggression that he or she carries out against teacher, headmaster and, ultimately, the law, are an expression of the aggression that was once felt towards the original authority—the parent. It is, indeed, almost a psychological cliché nowadays to describe stealing of property as a distortion of the original desire to take, violently, the parental love which seemed, even if only in fantasy, to be withheld.

The hated " they," the indeterminate occupants of a world which was, at one time, so hurtful that it could not be tolerated, the recipients of tongue-lashing criticism, and the victims of theft and the distress that is brought to them by the children they failed, this is a society and society has to protect itself. Revenge against " them " is met by revenge taken by " them " and thus the vicious circle is complete.

Yet it is one of " them " who has, ultimately, to play the role of sympathiser and healer, to provide that specific quality of comprehension and thus the possibility of rapport, which seemed to be missing in the person filially responsible. This person could be a Borstal instructor or an after-care worker, and it is he or she who turns out to be that necessary benign, yet firm parent-substitute, able to help some tortured adolescent away from a life of self-destroying petty crime.

In East Anglia there is an Approved School for delinquents of average and above average intelligence. The headmaster confirms that many of his most gifted charges, placed in a situation where they are at last faced with the consequences of their compulsively anti-social behaviour, are able to use that section of their intelligence which still remains free from distortion, to try to come to terms with themselves. But he also confirms that the really exceptionally gifted detainees, those with an I.Q. of 140 and over, do have this additional feeling of isolation that the gifted so often feel, and this proves yet another obstacle in the journey to an orthodox way of life. In fact, it seems often to be the case that this very gift of intelligence is the root cause of the problem. Resentful at a world which could not comprehend (parents, for instance, of far less intelligence) the child grew up determined to take revenge, grew up that is in years and in physique but not in feeling which remained fixated to the original time when the desire for revenge was initially experienced.

Another Approved School in the Home Counties specializes in High I.Q. delinquent girls, and these hurt and hurtful young women come, strangely it might seem, from good homes; homes where their parents tried everything in their power to stop the frightening progression towards delinquency and the inevitable result of such a progression. But these parents had failed originally, in some way or another, and they were the very people against whom the erring daughter was directing her delinquency. It is hardly to be expected that they could provide what was required when they were bound to be in the position of the enemy, whether they deserved it or not.

This particular Approved School is one of the few in the country which has the right to refuse admission, and great pains are taken at the time of selection to make sure that the future inmate will fit into a delicately balanced organization. The girl, at first, has been " filtered " through a Classifying Centre, and been given a number of tests, including one for intelligence. On arrival at the School, she is interviewed by the Headmistress, the Head's deputy, and the staff psychiatrist, all this to make certain that the young offender has the necessary qualifications and is of the necessary state of mind to enable her to fit into the " group " as it stands at her precise moment of entry. One disrupting influence is enough to ruin all the good and constructive work which is being carried out.

Many of the girls have been expelled from Grammar or well-known Independent Schools for one reason or another, so here they are given the chance, in an atmosphere of watchful and sympathetic discipline, to continue their education in only a slightly more limited way than if they had been able to remain, undisturbed, at their own Schools. In fact, the only marked limitation is due to the lack of laboratories, so the work concentrates on Art subjects. The teaching is of a high standard and if any of these " damaged " girls seems capable of benefiting by it, they can receive individual attention.

The going, of course, is difficult, because without exception, the girls are rebels, rebels against their families and thus in rebellion against the world of " them," the ones who cannot provide the love, the ones who don't understand, the often innocent promoters of self-destruction.

CASE HISTORY 1 " Sandy "

Still in her early 'teens, Sandy is beautiful to look at. With her long fair hair and green eyes, there is a slightly remote quality about her as she mixes, with apparent ease, among the other girls of the School. And those remarkable eyes look straight at you as you speak to her, seeming to give you all their attention until you wonder what Sandy is doing in a place that attempts to cater for the disturbed, the recalcitrant, and, in the eyes of the law, the criminal.

When she was a little girl, Sandy had this same quality. Her parents are wealthy and her father is at the top of his particular profession. Many visitors came to the house where they always admired the beautiful and, apparently, self-contained little girl.

Sandy has two brothers, and their early schooling was carefully planned. She, however, was merely sent to a school where the parents hoped she would be happy. They did not seem to realize that Sandy had an exceptional intelligence, and was worthy of the same consideration, so far as her education was concerned, as her brothers were receiving. Perhaps, as she was so attractive, she was automatically classed as a good-looker rather than a potential high-achiever. Many men do not like to equate beauty with brains, even in their own daughters.

As far back as she can remember, Sandy was a rebel. The lustrous hair and emerald eyes concealed a soul at war with the world. She may have *seemed* an integrated member of the family, but this she did not feel. There was always this quality of " difference "—a quality which still persists as she floats serenely amidst her rebellious contemporaries.

Sandy was bored at school. The lessons did not interest her, and eventually her parents were asked to take her away. She was sent to another school, with the same result, and another and another. Ultimately she ran away and instinctively gravitated to that group of nomadic questors, the " beatniks," sleeping rough, smoking reefers and watching with those cool green eyes sexual licence which, it so happened, did not interest her at all. And her way-out friends respected her for refusing to let her body be handled indiscriminately.

With the end of the mild weather, life became too much for her group. One or two stole and were caught, some disappeared, some even settled down to a job of work. The group, in fact, was a group no longer, and once again Sandy felt alone in the world; her promised land had been taken away from her.

At last the police found her and brought her back to her bewildered parents who, for the first time, realized the extent of the problem and knew they could not provide the right answer. Sandy was " committed for training " and there she remains today, one of a new group whose problems, she feels, matches her own and among whom, for the first time in her life, she feels at ease and wanted.

Her work is improving and, gradually, her interests are being captured. Given the continued stability of this background, there is every hope that she will learn to conquer her childish resentments, perhaps learn that others, too, have problems, even the despised parents, and above all learn to exploit her intelligence in such a way that she will find a niche for herself in a world that, hitherto, did not seem able to provide such a place.

CASE HISTORY 2 " Mark "

Mark is twenty six, a slightly built young man of exceptional charm. His fair hair is carefully brushed, his suit comes from a good tailor, his shirt is hand-made and his tie indicates that he has attended a University. In spite of his conventional appearance, his expression is quizzical and slightly mocking as though he were laughing at himself for trying to make a good impression, as if indeed knowing that he is making one. It is not so many years ago that he misused this valuable facility.

He is illegitimate, although he did not know this for certain until a year or two ago. His mother was dying when she told him, and even then, at the mature age of twenty four, his feelings of insecurity and bewilderment were such that he was overwhelmed and he rushed angrily out of the room to telephone a friend and pour out resentment against the mother whose only crime was that she had loved him and over-indulged him all her life. But by this time he was sufficiently on the way to genuine maturity to realize that these overwhelming feelings of rage were an expression of all his fears, doubts and daydreams about himself, and he was able to return to comfort his unfortunate mother in her last hours.

Like all illegitimate or adopted children who have not been told of their true origins, Mark had sensed a feeling of " difference " about himself, and the subtlety of this is very apparent when it is realized that his illegitimacy was purely technical inasmuch as he had merely been born out of wedlock. His parents, in fact, lived together without marrying before and, for a while, after his birth. Ultimately they did marry.

The family lived in the country where his father was a farm labourer. Because he was in a reserved occupation, the father was not called up for military service so they all remained together through the War. Thus Mark did not have to contend with the emotional upheaval that was the lot of all those children who were born at such a time and whose fathers were absent. He was reared, in fact, by two people who loved him, yet his sensitivity was such that this feeling of difference he experienced, for all its subtlety, must have produced the fantasies at the bottom of his disturbance.

American airmen were sometimes billeted on the family. These Mark remembers as strange romantic figures with clothes of much better quality and cut than he had ever seen before. Sometimes they spoiled him and gave him chocolate and other presents, and these too seemed much better, and were certainly bigger and more gaily wrapped than the wartime ration of chocolate obtainable from the village shops.

So Mark grew up quietly during a war which was showing him that people outside the family group could provide luxuries, while inside the family, there was only austerity. His parents did not think of him as particularly bright, but his continual questions had occasionally been thought of as " cute " by the Allied troops. Cuteness brought him gaily wrapped chocolate, but no satisfactory answers to the questions he asked continually.

The mixed Primary School to which he was first sent did not provide a continuation of the indulgences to which Mark was accustomed to receiving at home. Already he had learned that if he wanted something which was not forthcoming all he had to do was to scream, and lo and behold, the battle was won. But not at school. His temper tantrums did not endear him either to staff or fellow-pupils. He was ignored by both, and this was a frightening experience to a little boy who had received more than his share of attention. The youngsters around him, in fact, having decided that such behaviour did no good in the long run, went on with their plodding towards the difficult achievement of being " grown up." Mark did not have the chance to follow their example, because in his mother's eyes he continued to be right. Whatever good might have been done at school for the boy, was undone at home by the mother.

Yet he managed to do well at school for two reasons, the most important being his need to be top dog, and the second being his high intelligence. He had, in fact, learned to read even before he went to school, so it is no surprise that Mark ultimately won a place in the local Grammar school, although by this time his poor emotional adjustment to stress began to manifest itself, and he retreated into illness. This lasted no longer than it took for doctors to find out that the symptoms of polio, which Mark simulated so expertly, had no physical basis. Nevertheless, he succeeded in occupying the professional attentions of many people, and underwent exhaustive tests and spent several weeks in hospital before, abruptly, they discharged him.

At this point, it is important to delve further into Mark's background, because several elements point to an environment which was unusual. During the 30's, his father had become bankrupt, the result of the Depression, and had to relinquish his small shop. Yet the bankruptcy was talked about for many years as something to be proud of—a distortion of the true situation which must have had a great effect upon a highly intelligent and sensitive boy. Then again, the maternal grandmother had lived with his family for a while. She, it so happened, was the proprietor of a sweetshop, and this too, it seems, was a source of pride to the family. Perhaps it can be stated that there seemed to be a respect for the material things of life (the sweetshop and, negatively, the bankruptcy) and a curious, perhaps psychopathic, attitude towards financial responsibility, inasmuch as to most responsible people, to be bankrupt is no reason to feel proud. (It is interesting that to this day Mark has difficulties in remaining solvent, even though he seems established in a professional career and earns a good salary).

Thus Mark's formative years were influenced by a feeling that colour and satisfaction came from exotic sources—the gaily coloured richly flavoured chocolates from the American troops— the " glamour " of bankruptcy happening to a man who, by virtue of his trade, should have hardly been able to spell the word—so it is not surprising that exotic behaviour, rather than repel him, should seem to be a source of benevolence and gratification.

Mark was an attractive boy to look at, and his appearance, plus his growing instinct to savour the exotic, made him willing to submit to the unorthodox attentions of a man living in the next village. He took to this without guilt—it was the superficial aspect of novelty which interested him—and what child is not pleased to receive presents, or be taken on outings to the nearby coast? But his admirer soon lost interest, and this irked the boy, who wrote a letter of reproach to this man. " I don't remember whether I asked for money or not, I think I just wanted him to take notice of me again. I didn't like to think that he had got over me so easily " says Mark, recollecting the episode, but the letter roused panic and the recipient, fearful of being blackmailed, went to the police. Thus Mark appeared before the local Magistrate and was put on probation, a state of affairs which bewildered him because the whole affair meant little to him compared to the excess of fuss surrounding it. His resentment was misinterpreted by the Probation Officer as a dislike for all authority, while the boy was intrigued by the young probationers he found himself mixing with. These aggressive young offenders managed to upset him by their outspoken dislike of his continued education at School (where, incidentally, his attention had not been captured by the low level of the syllabus, and he was completing no more work than was enough to keep him out of trouble).

Thus Mark's period of probation began, and it was at this time that he became fascinated by the ritual and colour of the Roman Catholic church, the richly embroidered robes of the Priests, and the fact that boys of his age could become Servers and thus members of an " in " group. His schoolwork continued at its level of under-achievement, and he passed only four G.C.E. subjects, so he could no longer stay on. Further resentment was the result of this.

He started work, and one unsatisfactory job followed another. None of them interested him—they were all so dull, so colourless, but in all fairness, he did teach himself to type feeling that this was a way to the " better " life that he felt he deserved, but could not identify.

Fascinated as always by ritual and the mysterious, he joined a fringe religion in which ritual figured prominently. The Leader was a rich man, easily flattered by the new and good-looking convert. For the first time, Mark saw what money could really buy —he was taken out to meals in fashionable London restaurants and he went back to the Leader's house where silver and gold ornaments lay around as if no more valuable than cheap pottery. All this he loved, this was the way to live—but he felt a need to dress the part and it was impossible to do this on a wage of less than four pounds a week.

He began to run up bills at various shops. After all, his patron often said " put this down to my account " in relation to his own purchases, and Mark was merely imitating him. The only difference, of course, being the fact that as he had no money to pay, ultimately, for the purchases, he had to take the understandable precaution of giving a false name!

Ready money then became a problem, so he began to steal. This continued for quite a while, and the source was the presents to the " faithful " that his rich patron was accustomed to making. Perhaps various items were noticed to be missing from time to time, but this trusting man did not connect these losses with his new convert (who had gone out of his way to inform him of a recent inheritance from an aunt).

The time came, however, when Mark over-reached himself. A snuffbox he had filched was of great value and the antique dealer to whom he offered it became suspicious and contacted the police. The whole structure began to rock—other members remembered they had not seen certain pieces of jewellery for a while, shop-keepers began to make enquiries with the result that Mark found himself in serious trouble.

Again he was bewildered. Didn't people he admired run up bills? To be bankrupt was something of which to be proud, wasn't it? But the Magistrate did not follow this reasoning, neither was he acquainted with the distorted background which made such reasoning possible, and Mark was sent for Borstal training.

It was here that his intelligence was used, constructively, for the first time, for it was here that he found people who both understood and accepted him, and he began to learn that certain actions produce certain results. On the same level he realized that if he won approval he would be released sooner, so he set out to do this. And in this restrictive and disciplining atmosphere, his work began to give him satisfaction at last.

At the end of eighteen months he was released on Licence and helped to enter a Technical College where he soon passed three "A" level subjects and several more at "O" level. He then applied for, and was accepted by, a provincial University where, finally, he took a Second Class Honours degree. After coming down, he went into journalism and turned out to be good at human interest stories. He had learned to become a success by his own efforts.

Will his life continue to deepen and consolidate? Or is there still the possibility that an impulse will arise at a time when he is monetarily low and he will enter into a financial contract which he cannot fulfil? " My bank manager " says Mark " understands me! " and at the risk of seeming uncharitable there is a feeling of unease at these ominous words because there was always that time when to be bankrupt was to be different, to be " better " and to be colourful.

9

The Bridges Experiment and others

WE live in the time of conformity. The ever-growing complexity of life necessitates an increase in the number of rules
by which we need to abide. During adolescence, the external manifestations of such a need are felt, by the adolescent, to be an
unbearable infringement of his right to be himself, and a kind of
anarchy is practised for a while. Probably it is seen at its (legal)
extreme in the current fashion for boys to adopt hair styles and
ornamentation hitherto regarded, in Western civilization, as
peculiar to the opposite sex. Many girls, likewise, seem anxious
not to advertise their feminine charms by conventionally feminine
modes of apparel, preferring to wear their hair short and their
bootees long! Ultimately the need to break the old rules dies with
the realization that you can be yourself, inside, without having to
show it in rebelliousness outside.

But the other side of the coin is fear—fear of that which is
different and alien. Perhaps adolescent anarchy is, sometimes, an
outward rebellion against conscious fear of non-conformity, but on
a less involved level of consideration, it cannot be denied that, on
the whole, many people are frightened to a greater or lesser degree
when they encounter something which is beyond them and which,
therefore, they do not understand.

It is an irrational fear, which can deny the gifted child his
due recognition, for a rare mind can be felt, by one who does not
possess its equal yet is there to guide it, as a threat. This con-
stitutes a very real problem in the teaching of gifted children,
and therefore it is realized that it is just as important for a teacher
to be " trained " to accept brilliance in his pupils, even be

stimulated by it, as it is for the brilliant pupil to be placed, educationally, in an ambience most conducive to the furtherance of his potential.

It is the rigidity of the educational pattern (matching only too often the rigidity of the minds of those hired to do the educating) which stimulated Dr. S. A. Bridges, senior lecturer in Education at the Brentwood Training College for Teachers, to attempt a breakthrough in such a way that both pupils and teachers enter into an inter-dependent relationship, so that not only are the specific gifts of the child catered for but, in the very process of catering, the teacher too learns to open *his* mind, and allows it to develop.

" September for the High I.Q. child is a foolish month to be born in " says Dr. Bridges, caustically delivering a verbal assault on a system which makes such an eccentric statement a pronouncement of irrefutable logic! " It may mean unless the authorities are enlightened and flexible and, in addition, have plenty of school places, that such a child, instead of at least being with his chronological age group with whom he has little enough in common, will be with children almost a year younger, a placing which will provide him with yet an additional handicap." Thus Dr. Bridges decided to do what he could to give the gifted children in Primary Schools around the College a chance to meet other gifted children, to experiment in ways of teaching them, and to give some of the students at Brentwood a chance to teach gifted children.

Teachers of such children do not of necessity have to be of exceptionally high I.Q. themselves so long as they are ready to acknowledge that the children they teach are more intelligent than themselves. After all, his life experience means that a teacher has something important to offer. He can help too in the creation of the right climate for learning, he can recommend books to read, plays to see, music to listen to, and above all supply the relationship, based on intellectual appreciation, which will make it possible for his gifted charge to break away from any intellectual narrowness which might exist in the child's own family, and seek extra-familial outlets for the exchange of ideas that he needs. It is, indeed, a kind of humility that Brentwood attempts to inculcate in its students.

In September 1964, some children were chosen from four different Primary Schools close to Brentwood College, all of whom had reached the "ceiling" of a verbal reasoning test. They were brought together at the College for one afternoon a week throughout the term and taught in small groups by selected students under Dr. Bridges' supervision. The students, too, had been chosen, primarily for their enthusiasm of the scheme, and then for flexibility of mind, and the ability to accept the children's achievements. The young pupils were divided into two groups, all of them with I.Q.'s between 138 and 170 plus and had been tested prior to selection either by George Robb, the Senior Psychologist to the Essex Education Committee, or a trusted member of his staff.

In the first instance, selection had occurred through the Headmasters of the four Primary Schools concerned, who had become interested in the Pilot Study and wished to co-operate in the main scheme. They had seen the parents and had explained that their child was considered gifted and that it would be beneficial for the child to attend a special class for one half day a week.

The two groups consisted of (a) those children who, at the time of selection, were between the ages of eight and nine and (b) those who, at the age of selection, were in their tenth year but had not reached the age of ten.

At the time of writing, the experiment continues. The groups remain together throughout the afternoon, and one of the most striking elements is the enormous pleasure expressed by these children at the discovery that there are others like themselves! To be gifted is, often, to be isolated and one heard frequently the same complaint . . . "No-one wants to talk about the things I'm interested in. They think I'm a show-off . . ." The children had not been given the chance to realize that others, two or three years older than themselves, *would* have been interested in knowing them. The structured world of school and childhood prevents this age-mixing, and high intelligence and immense curiosity in the external world are felt as "strange" by less gifted contemporaries and the unlucky owner of a gifted mind comes up against the cruelty of rejection.

For the first part of the afternoon, the two groups participate in one of two activities: Arts and Crafts, and Special P.E. and creative drama. Afterwards, it is English activities (culminating in free discussion) with the alternative choice of Maths, including the use of special apparatus.

The students who take part in the Bridges experiment are in the second and third years of their three year training, but not in their final term, as during this they must devote all their time to their own studies. They regard the opportunity they have been given as a privilege and a challenge and, under direction, are encouraged to try out ideas of their own. As a result, the male student teaching Maths formulated a third and more successful method of dealing with a problem after one of his nine years old girl pupils had suggested an alternative to that which he had originally put forward. This particular man is himself outstanding and perhaps after some experience in an ordinary school, he will be able to devote himself, in his turn, to the stimulating problem of teaching the gifted.

Dr. Bridges' scheme was helped considerably by the enlightened attitude of George Robb who has been interested in the question of the " handicap " of brilliance for some years. Robb remembers a child of six who was referred to him, and who seemed to be turning into an isolate, mixing less and less with the others in his class. It transpired that the child was discouraged because the other children were not interested in the startling discovery he had made, all by himself, that if you look at a spoon one way you get an inverted image, but if you look at it the other way, you don't! When tested, this child's I.Q. was found to be over 200 and ultimately, an enlightened education authority made it possible for this extraordinary youngster to receive the special educational attention he needed at a school where the headmaster is concerned with meeting the needs of gifted children.

Another boy, referred at the age of eleven, was described by his teacher as " a smart-aleck who won't work except at nature study and then he wants to run the lesson." The boy was found to have an I.Q. of 175 and had been thoroughly bored with the work he had been set. In the process he had provoked the hostility of his teacher who had failed to recognize such outstanding ability.

Essex, indeed, is one of the more educationally enlightened counties and in 1966 is to commence building the first residential school in the country run by a local authority, for the treatment and education of high I.Q. maladjusted children, both boys and girls, between the ages of eleven and eighteen, and whose intelligence, measured in the Binet scale, will be at least 130.

The Bridges experiment does not contain all the answers to the problem it attempts to solve, otherwise it would not be an experiment. For instance, it seems a pity that little if any contact with parents is pursued, because having a gifted child is to have a child with a problem, even if he is not a " problem child." While he is attending the weekly special class, it would seem a great opportunity to find out more about the kind of family into which such a child is born, to see if there are any common factors, with similar families other than those few which are already known. The authors suggest also that closed-circuit televising of this class would give the teachers in their basic school the unique opportunity of studying the behaviour of their young charges when amongst their intellectual peers.

On the day that the authors visited Brentwood, they were able to be present from the time that the children arrived. As they all met, they seemed to blossom with a new exuberance, and there was the feeling of participating in some exciting expedition. Among Group Two is nine years old Colin, tall for his age, slightly built with dark hair and an alert manner. Colin's father is a graduate, teaching sixth form physics, and the boy's interests also lay in this direction. He came top in the number test on selection, getting 44 out of a possible 55, but is weaker on the verbal side, getting only 19 out of a possible 35. Nevertheless, his I.Q. is 170 plus and he is relaxed and ready to learn from others, student teachers and pupils alike. Janet, on the other hand, although she has an I.Q. of 163 plus, is less confident. Just before selection she had become miserable and unhappy, saying she didn't want to go to school any more as no one wanted to play with her. She was, of course, up against this great problem of loneliness through lack of meeting her contemporaries on common intellectual ground. She is improving, although much hurt seems to have been done and manifests itself in her hesitance in answering questions to which she obviously knows the answers. But her own brilliance was suspect to her—hadn't it taken away the possibility of making friends?

All the children in the group showed the insatiable curiosity and eager inventiveness of their kind. When told of some of the machinery that Leonardo had invented, they wanted to " have a bash " themselves, and here at Brentwood they are given every encouragement to put to practical use the intelligence that, in adverse circumstances, could so easily amount to an unfortunate blessing.

" It wouldn't be any good the cows saying they hadn't been here, would it! " remarked a four years old boy, having walked through a field minus cows, but dotted with cow pats. Apart from the incredible trenchancy of such an observation in one so young, the imaginative touch of implying that cows can talk is of a charm that could only be attributed to a child.

The need to allow, in a child, these childish fantasies and yet, side by side, promote the growth of achievement and worldliness, is here seen in an exemplary way, and this child is lucky in being the pupil of a school where the Headmistress is very concerned with the nurturing of intellectual potential in gifted children, but not to the exclusion of their imaginative life.

The outstanding element of this Independent School, is the awareness of climate, the climate, that is, in which such a child as that quoted can expand or to use the educational term, extend. It so happens that the pupils, whose ages range from three and a half to fourteen, are mainly children of professional parents, some of whom are widely travelled. Souvenirs of these travels are seen in the classrooms and occasionally, when displayed, the classrooms present a picture of riotous exoticism, with primitive weapons and other objects of craftsmanship all over the place.

Each individual item, be it a carved dagger or a wooden eating bowl, represents the beginning of an investigation into its use, its country, and even its development into some modern form. But such concern with " colour " might create a feeling in the reader that this is an organization run by cranks! Far from it—the School was founded as the demonstration school of the Fröbel Educational

Institute, and is in close touch with all modern educational trends, and practises them whenever possible. The " climate for growth " angle is merely an adjunct to the basic scholastic curriculum, and is the natural outcome of dealing with imaginative and gifted pupils, by an enlightened Head and staff.

Possible confirmation of the importance of " colour " in a child's life, can be given, indeed, by one of the authors whose recall of childhood is notoriously deficient, but who does, however, remember an incident which occurred at the age of seven. At the Primary School he attended, he, as a new pupil, was singled out by a teacher (for some now forgotten felicity) and given a remarkable ugly carved wooden model of an Indian elephant! But it seemed wondrous then, and has never been forgotten. Unfortunately, it was an isolated incident in a childhood of almost total misunder-standing, and therefore it seems worth recording that such a departure from the conventional has been remembered for almost thirty-five years. Would that there had been more such departures!

Southend is hardly a place where, one would think, unusually progressive work is being done in the field of educating the gifted child. The image of the town, one of whelks, beer, and kiss-me-quick hats, derives from the famous Golden Mile of esplanade, and the far-from-Golden miles of muddy deposit lapped by the even-further-from-marine waters of the Thames estuary. But it is not for nothing that the children of Southend seem hardly to notice the week-end and seasonal invasion of tourists wearing those funny little hats! They have their own life to lead and Essex, after all, is their county, one of the most educationally minded of all the counties.

It so happens that, due to its size, the County Borough of Southend has its own Education Authority, but some of the enlightened attitude of the " mother " county must have rubbed off onto Southend, and the Head of one of its Junior Schools, is one of the more advanced thinkers in the education of gifted children.

This man is an idealist, and believes that at school gifted children should have a room of their own, or at least a section of such a room, where they can be left to their own devices. He points out an element in such children that would seem to be of some importance in dealing with them—that of impatience to communicate their constant and, to them, exciting new insights. Such internal discoveries often happen with the speed of an impulse, and this is followed by the compulsive need to communicate the discovery. In fact, suggests this idealist, a teacher of similar gifts to the child should be available at any minute of the day, ready to be approached and able to communicate constructively with the child at " the moment of truth." However, he agrees that such a state of affairs is hardly likely to exist outside the realms of fantasy!

In addition to a room for the highly intelligent and gifted, he believes there is a need for a half-time teacher (at least) in every Primary School, with a special interest in such children. In the meantime, special tasks are devised to cater for the gifted group in his school. The class was asked to investigate the Prittle Brook (a local stream) and to follow its course from its source, through the town until it came out in a park. In order to do this, the children had to learn to read an ordnance survey map, and the " voyage of discovery " extended to the identification of plants, birds and small animals (by means of reference books). They learned to find a position by measurement and then went on to invent means of triangulating and drawing their own sketch maps to scale. At the end, they learned to present all that they had caught, read and preserved in such a way that it made sense to other people. In other words, these children, all under the age of eleven, had carried out a piece of research in the best professional tradition, working as a team, yet each according to his inclination and ability.

No great discoveries were ever made by men who were travelling well-trodden paths, and the Head's intention is to create ever-widening fields of enquiry for his pupils who will, in the process, be encouraged to follow their own bent and take a route which, under expert guidance, is indeed a personal voyage of discovery. All too often, when they get to University, such children finish up not with a First but with an ordinary degree of no special merit, not because they could not do it, but because there was never enough excitement in the early days to make then employ their resources to the full, a kind of under-achievement which is difficult to overcome.

One of the lecturers of a London University course on the teaching of the gifted is at present Head of a Junior Mixed School catering for a recently built estate, close to Greenwich. This is one of the most exciting suburbs of London, dominated by the pre-served " Cutty Sark " and redolent with a maritime atmosphere that will be forever enhanced by the constant and stately procession of large and small boats of all countries and all denominations, up and down the Thames.

With the formal layout of its river-mist haunted park, its gracious architecture, boatworkers shops (compasses, binoculars, rigging), the Royal Naval College, Maritime Museum and, in contrast, a shabby and slum-ridden area of murky air and murkier tenements, with a foot-tunnel under the Thames connecting one of the most colourful areas of any great city to one of the least (the Isle of Dogs—but squalor too has its own poetry!) Greenwich offers, in its own " climate " the unique and sparklingly active ambience that occurs in any of the world's great ports.

The School in question stands in the middle of a brash new estate which itself has been built on an area recently reclaimed from marshland. In contrast to its bustling seaport-like neighbour, the Estate has yet to create a tradition of living of its own, and in the presence of an exceptional Headmaster, it contains the man to inculcate such a tradition. Already his pupils are passing on their enthusiasms to their parents, and a vital sense of discovery is being established. A ten years old girl, having gone on a School expedition to study the Roman remains at Lullingstone was fired to the extent of persuading her parents to take her on a second visit. " Mother and father were very impressed, they had never heard of it before " she later reported!

Almost as new as the Estate which it serves, the School, when opened, did not " stream " children in their first two years, i.e. the seven and eight years old were divided into groups by age and not by intelligence based on reports from their previous Infant and Junior Schools. With three hundred and sixty new arrivals, the important thing was to discover newly, individual capabilities. The nine and ten years old were " streamed " for two years after the School started, but now even that has ceased.

Unlike many of his colleagues in the profession, the Head believes that this is of definite help in selecting the gifted for every teacher is then forced to examine every child and is not influenced by the fact that a pupil might be in " C " stream. Such a child can still be gifted, but as yet unrecognized.

At first it was the less able children who received additional help, and this has been followed by the same sort of supplementary help being given to gifted children. The children are enabled to work at their own pace, in groups of their own kind and for at least some of the time, in something out of the ordinary in which they are particularly interested.

Any specialized interest can be made the focal point for a project, and these projects will last any time from a fortnight to a year. In such projects the gifted are given the opportunity to act as leaders. They are given more difficult assignments, too, such as having the responsibility for undertaking the library research, controlling the rest of the children, and so on. The libraries, in fact, are strikingly used by the children who, coming from a working class background, would not be expected to gravitate instinctively towards reading for pleasure.

When the new Public Library was opened by the Mayor in 1965, he pointed out that it was the children, rather than their parents, who were the readers although in all fairness, such a facility, available to people who had not been brought up to derive pleasure from reading, cannot be expected to be taken advantage of overnight. In fact, now that books are available, it may well be that parents will read more because their interest has been aroused by their children, and in this way, the life of the whole district will be enriched by the vision and drive of a local Headmaster and his staff.

On the estate from which most of the children come, there is an encampment. Some of the families are true gypsies, some diddicoy, and some are fairground people. Few of their children have had much schooling because families are constantly on the move. No-one knows, even, how many children there are in individual families, because they either hide or are hidden whenever the " School man " pays his time-to-time visits. In many instances, the Head seems to have won the confidence of these families, and now an ever increasing number of these nomadic children spend a few months with him before they move on. Some are illiterate, but although they cannot read or write, they talk vividly, handle money confidently and know its value.

Phyllis is one such child who usually spends the winter months at this school. She is an unusually able girl whose physical health is not very good due, perhaps, to the circumstances under which the family live. Soon they will be off on the road again until the dark days and autumn mists drive them back to a permanent camping site. Another child, Maxime, who has been an occasional pupil, has recently been awarded a Grammar School place in Essex. She, in fact, must be very gifted for her family are seldom more than ten days in any one place and her mother says it seems hardly worth while sending her to school, for as soon as she settles in, the family are off again. Maxime excels in all written work, in drama, and in her general confidence and assurance. She is a leader and a natural performer in all music and drama work. One can only hope that her circumstances will not prevent her occupying the place in life to which her gifts entitle her.

The school is showing that, with new thinking, education for the gifted can be given within an orthodox framework if the system is not too rigid. It is to be hoped that his pupils who succeed in achieving Grammar School places will receive the same sensitive handling, for when such a child has finally been recognized, he will be even more in need of the sort of encouragement which produced the initial results.

The above are just a few of the largely " unknown " pockets of enlightened instruction that exist throughout the country. Here and there, isolated groups of similar value are carrying out this essential work, but the instigators so often feel, mistakenly, that theirs is a voice in the wilderness, for they are unaware of the attempts of others. A form of liaison would seem to be urgently required, so that the efforts of all are available to all and, ultimately, draw the attention of the powers-that-be in the headquarters of educational administration.

10

A Second Chance

IN this technological age, when very high intelligence is at a premium, it is ironical that early manifestations of such intelligence, rather than bringing joy to the teacher, can bring frustration. But we should make it clear that in this case we are dealing with something more than brilliance. The problem, in fact, is what to do with a youngster whose intelligence is such that he or she can be assessed as a potential genius.

Time and again, during the course of the authors' research, they found authorities anxious *not* to denigrate teachers. "Give them the chance and they will rise to the occasion" was a common answer to the question "should exceptionally gifted children be instructed by exceptionally gifted teachers?"

To a large extent the authorities agree that, in many cases, teachers are forced into being, themselves, under-achievers inasmuch as they are dealing with children of limited intelligence. But, of course, so many of us feel we are capable of doing far better work than that which we are given the opportunity to carry out. And we may well be right! But the time comes when something materializes which creates, almost, its own rules, demands a level of perception and performance that we cannot rise to and with which, if we have a necessary sense of humility, we are forced to admit we are inadequate to deal. In the case of a teacher, that "something" could be a child whose intelligence is such, that it is beyond assessment. The child who is a near genius.

A teacher longs for the stimulation of a bright and lively mind, but then again, the packer in an electrical components factory longs to win the football pools. Occasionally such a man wins the pools

In retrospect at Carisbrooke Castle

On the spot at
The Needles Lighthouse

Interpretation and creation in the arts

—and how does he react? Nine time out of ten, he'll buy a few things he has not been able, in the past, to afford, and that is that. What is more, these purchases will rarely be such that by virtue of owning them, he will be placing himself outside the range of contact with his neighbours and friends. The money, in fact, is "wisely invested" and there it stays, growing uselessly. It is, simply, too big a sum to be handled comfortably by the owner.

Likewise the sum of intelligence handed, one could say, to an undiscerning teacher. He is simply not equipped to deal with a mind that extends far beyond his own capacity. It is "too big" to be handled comfortably and wisely by him. "What can I do with this pupil? Nobody here can do justice to him, so where can he go?" is the often heard cry. Well, there is always Millfield School, provided, of course, that room can be found in this remarkable establishment.

Millfield School, appropriately, is situated in an area which, for well over a thousand years, has been a seat of learning. Here, in the pastoral Isle of Avalon, legendary home of King Arthur, the Monks of Glastonbury had formed a centre of teaching, and from their wisdom, knowledge was spread far beyond the Abbey. The School itself is in the small town of Street, only a few miles from Glastonbury, and within sight of Glastonbury Tor, a green mound which dominates the landscape. It is housed in an old building constructed of the local warm and golden stone—in great contrast to the rash of brightly painted Nissen huts which flank the approach. Why should the most expensive Public School in England still be using Nissen huts as classrooms twenty years after the Second World War? True enough, they are gradually giving way to the latest type of prefab, but the fact that they exist here is an indication of the emphasis that is put on the need for numerous small classrooms where groups of boys, never more than ten or, at the most, twelve at a time, can be alone with their tutor, for Millfield houses a collection of astonishingly gifted pupils whose collective brain power can hardly be calculated.

Perhaps the most impressive single element about Millfield is the headmaster (R. J. O. Meyer, M.A.) a man whose zeal springs

97

4

straight from the undying tradition of English fanatics, a tradition which has produced many revolutions, both bloody and bloodless. He is known as " Boss," and it is the belief of Boss that children should have the education best suited to them whatever the cost; and that the highly intelligent child should have the chance to develop early so that he will not have to waste time " unlearning," or become unhappy, even maladjusted, through frustration.

Meyer is tall, well over average height, a connoisseur of the good things of life. He speaks slowly at first and then, if the subject interests him (and anything to do with gifted children interests him) the words pour out, he runs his hands through his hair until he resembles an earnest and learned parrot . . .

. . . " Harch of the American National Broadcasting Company was over to see me . . . ' the best teaching in the worst possible classrooms ' was what he was after . . . I showed him into one of the Nissen huts where the door was hanging off the hinges . . . there was this incredible six years old Australian boy and I'd already decided how to show the boy off, what my question was to be . . . the presiding master had already been briefed . . . we already knew the answer (we thought) . . . this boy . . . he'd come from Australia because otherwise he'd have had to wait six years to enter his next school . . . already he was skating through the Latin questions we'd once given a brilliant fifteen years old pupil who, later, won a Scholarship to Cambridge before he was seventeen . . . ' I've got a question for you, John ' said the teacher ' how old are you? ' ' Six years, so many months, so many weeks, so many days . . .' ' How many days then to your next birthday but five? ' ' One thousand, one hundred and thirty-five ' came the answer, pat. It sounded mad . . . I couldn't look at Harch . . . ' You've let the School down John ' reproached the master, but John hadn't! It was I. John was born in a leap year . . . he was correct . . ."

Meyer's study is lined with books, there are books piled on chairs, books lying on the floor. Piles of letters all over the place, too, from all over the world, from parents making enquiries about the length of the waiting list, from educationalists with whom he has long and, sometimes, acrimonious battles over his teaching methods (methods constantly in a state of flux, as he learns more about the subject).

Millfield is one of the few Public Schools where the child with the really high I.Q. will get a place, no matter whether the parents can afford the fees or not. In addition some local authorities are prepared to cover the fees if they think a particular child's needs are best met here.

But it isn't always as easy as that. Many who control the purse-strings are convinced that such children can be catered for within the normal school system and come to no harm by working, for instance, in a class of forty children with a wide range of I.Q.'s.

This can be the case, provided the teacher is himself excep-tional and aware, also, of the potentialities of each child. It must be remembered that the ordinary group intelligence tests do not always reveal the unusually brilliant child to his best advantage— he may well have become bored halfway through the test!

... " Some of the boys ... I can't get money for them, so what do I do? I beg, beg ... I had one parent who said he had never given in his life, not even to his wife or children. I knew he could afford it so I refused to take his children till he agreed to help ... it was a challenge ... he said that I boast I can do all sorts of things, like producing international athletes, and so on ... he bet me that I couldn't ... I told him to name a child, and that if he won the bet, I'd refund the fees he paid ... he never got his money back—he named two children, one became a famous Olympics athlete, the other played Cricket for Somerset ... this parent told me he enjoyed losing money in this way, and he'd make a similar bet! ... Sometimes it's not only begging but gentle pressure with it ... invite the rich to help me in the work of helping the poor because it will make them happier and also help the country (say I) ... I hate to admit it, but some of them call me Robin Hood ... a very well known business magnate rang up and wanted me to take his son for Edgarley, then Millfield and then the best house at Eton. I told him I could enter the boy for Edgarley and Millfield, if given reasonable time, but for Eton the boy would have to be registered at birth ... that should be easy enough was the reply, he's not due to be born for a week! In fact, it was a girl, and so was the next one, but at last he rang up to announce he was the father of a son. I said I'd do him the favour he wanted if he'd do me one . . . I asked him to help me financially to place a bright boy from this man's locality, he agreed to meet him . . . we arrived and he liked the boy, but said he'd prefer it to be the son of one of his employees . . . but this *is* such a boy, I told him, but it isn't surprising that he forgot the name of one of his Company's bricklayers, and now the boy's thirteen and already got his ' O ' levels. That's how it's done! " . . .

With modern teaching methods, children, even in a large class, can be divided into groups and taught at different rates of progress, but " Boss " holds firmly to the opinion that children should be with their intellectual peers for at least part of the day. Competition is a natural attribute of the healthy human animal, and a young student is stimulated if he meets (as he does at Millfield, probably for the first time) others who are at least as able, and in some cases superior, to himself.

This does not mean, however, that because there are, at present, seventy-three boys and girls at Millfield with I.Q.'s ranging from 145 to 192 (and nineteen at the Prep School at nearby Edgarley) that Millfield is a school only for children of high intelligence such as are found in America (e.g. Hunter College). Meyer believes that, apart from the time actually spent in academic work, children definitely benefit by being with others of their own age and of widely differing intelligences and backgrounds. For this reason, twenty-five percent of places throughout the School are kept for boys who may never pass more than one or two G.C.E.'s at " O " level, and who follow a much more practical syllabus, including maintenance of farm machinery, visits to local farms and actual outdoor work.

It is interesting to note that many of the high I.Q. children are also interested in these subjects and although, owing to their particular academic programme, they do not have much time to devote to such a subject as Botany, an interest in it can take a most practical form . . .

JAMES (aged 14) " There are only forty day boys and I suppose it's a disadvantage to be one if one wants to hold office in the House or the School for that matter, but I don't mind. I like being at home for weekends and doing what I like for two days. This year I'm making an ecological study of an orchard, and I can spend a good deal of time at weekends with the trees and looking at things, and I like Botany too. I went to a P.N.E.U. School before I went to Edgarley and we did Nature Study there and of course we have always lived in the country. I'm fourteen years and two months and I don't really know what I want to do. You see, I like Maths and Art and Botany about equally. Of course one has to have exams, but I like doing things on my own. Actually up to now I've got ' O ' levels in Maths and English Language and English Literature and French, Latin, Geography and one other. Now I suppose I'll do my ' A's ' . . ."

The astonishing range of subjects, themselves sub-divided into the various levels suited to those minds concerned with them, raises all sorts of questions. The complexity of pattern of this syllabus emerges with clarity in a short interview with the Assistant Director of Studies, who is himself responsible for the very complicated time-table:

Q. Is it so that teaching occurs in Groups rather than classes?

A. Yes, with a maximum of ten or maybe twelve children. This is supplemented by special teaching which means that individual difficulties are noted and mistakes can be corrected. One of the main features is the elastic time-table which has been so devised that each pupil's time-table is completely individual, with a choice of subjects at any required stage. Planned in this way, a pupil's work is easy to review.

Q. Is there a basic point from which there is individual departure?

A. Yes, we have devised a basic grid to include, for instance, English and Maths. Every group is doing something " away " from the basic grid, Divinity, for example, for

Moslems: and the languages become distinctly variable, Latin in place of French, and for the Orientals, any of the Oriental languages. We can deal with forty-two languages. The language staff are supplemented by specialists.

Q. Does the fact that the boys come from varied backgrounds create problems?

A. Neither colour nor class exist here as a problem. The " mixing " is absolute.

Q. What happens to children who take their " O " levels very early?

A. In the case of the very young, we lay on additional sub-jects. They may do three languages, or an additional science. One boy has just been given a scheme of work in both biology and chemistry before he enters University in October.

Q. There are a certain number of girl students. Do you encounter problems relating to Sex?

A. No. We lay on talks which are well done, and occur with regularity. There are, of course, only eighty-two girls (at the moment) out of a total of six hundred and sixty-six pupils, but they do the same work as the boys in every way.

Perhaps this is the place to comment on the question of girls in a boys' school. Millfield certainly does not call itself co-educational, neither is it in any sense a " mixed " school. But the fact remains that there are over a hundred girls in the School. Meyer says that it is impossible to keep them out. Most of them have brothers or cousins at Millfield and had demanded to come. Alternatively, having failed at other schools, they had been brought to Millfield by their parents, quickly assessed the atmosphere and simply refused to go anywhere else!

It isn't surprising that their presence creates no emotional problems, for they are all girls of high I.Q., greedy for learning or of considerable ability at games and this (according to Meyer) is why no acute problems arise. In any case, strict rules exist relating to boys and girls being alone together, and there is the threat of instant dismissal if these rules are broken. It seems that the threat in itself is enough to damp down adolescent passion. Nothing here follows an accepted pattern, and in an atmosphere conventionally the opposite to " conducive," miracles of learning and achievement occur.

" Boss " was not given his affectionate nickname for nothing. At Millfield there is definitely one Captain, definitely one ship. He has built the School from nothing, seen it grow, and is determined that no outstanding child be turned away, if the parents want it to come and, more important still, if Meyer and the child decide between them, that this is the place where it will be happy.

Interviews go on throughout the year. It can start with a frantic telephone call from some parent: " My son is making no progress at his Prep School. The head says he doesn't stand a chance of getting into X . . . The boy says he's bored at school. How can a boy of eleven be bored? " But Meyer knows that boredom is the most striking symptom of under-achievement, so he is not deterred.

An interview between parent and Head is the best part of a day spent in mutual assessment. There are talks in the book-littered study, walks around the grounds, watching children from all over the world participating in all kinds of activity, from the more formal team games to archery and horse-riding. A psychological test is given to the prospective pupil—the Terman Merrill form " L " is used with projective tests if the psychologist thinks them necessary. Diagnostic tests are also given in mathematics, and these range from simple mechanical calculation to problems where comprehension plays a major part. Similar tests are given in English, and these show up the gaps in basic learning which occur when children move home (and school) for whatever reason.

More than a few pupils at Millfield come from Service families. Nowadays, of course, children are not sent home for their schooling if their father is serving abroad, in which case there is always the advantage of being within visiting distance of their parents, though teaching standards in overseas schools occasionally leave much to be desired. Then again, in the case of a child who does *not* come home for his schooling, there is the constant problem of being unable to stay more than a few years at any one school, for the father may be posted to a different country and, of course, the child follows. Going to a new school may mean starting again at the bottom, and once again the possibility occurs of boredom and under-achievement. Thus, for such boys and girls, and many others, Millfield does indeed offer a second chance or, more accurately, their first chance to use the exceptional brains with which they have been endowed.

As will have been noted from the short interview with the Director of Studies, many pupils do pass their " O " and " A " levels two or three years earlier than the time they would have sat for them at more conventional establishments. At Millfield this is considered to be in the child's best interests. He then has time to concentrate on the subjects at which he is weakest or, perhaps, learn Russian or any of the forty-two modern and classical languages which are available for instruction. These include some that one might not think of as practical in the modern world, such as Tibetan, but in addition, pupils who might spend their adult life in Asia, would also learn Chinese, Japanese, Hindu, Malay, Thai and Urdu. Three African languages can be learned, including Swahili, while from the twelve European languages, the pupil might select, in addition to the Russian he has already chosen, Swedish or modern Greek.

The time between the passing of the exams necessary to enable a pupil to go to University, and his being old enough actually to go there, is sometimes a problem. Many of the boys and girls elect to stay on at the School and fill out their education, and it is in such instances that the wide range of subjects and sports which can be learned is of exceptional benefit. Some, however, do spend a year or two abroad, occasionally able to do work beneficial to the inhabitants of " emergent " countries. This, naturally, can deepen awareness of world problems, and brings concomitant advantages to the pupil if his future studies are in the realms of the humanities ...
ROBERT (aged 13) ... " I like chess and studying criminal law. I like real life cases and books by Lustgarten and Furneaux where

they have violent results. I think there should be stricter control over the sale of guns otherwise more people are going to get shot . . . I had eight 'O' levels when I came into the senior school last September and now I am working for three 'A' levels, Maths, Latin and History. I hope to take my Maths combined this coming Summer and the others the Summer after when I will be just fifteen. Then I'll have a year or two to study for a Scholarship before going into University. After I have my degree I'd like to be a teacher, that's the thing I want to do. I've always wanted to do that. I like people . . ."

For all the fact that the atmosphere at Millfield would seem to be one of rarefied intellectualism, pupils are constantly and deliberately brought " down to earth." One of Meyer's innovations is a weekly period, between tea and supper, spent on what is referred to as " public works." In other words, service to the community in which the pupils are living. This includes window cleaning and wood cutting, tidying up the workshops and weeding the gardens. " Boss " knows that many of his boys will rise to positions of great influence in their own countries, and believes that not only should they learn that privilege brings responsibility, but that manual work also has a dignity of its own. A bricklayer in some far Eastern country will not be despised by a future administrator educated at Millfield!

A real surprise is the Headmaster's firm belief that his pupils should join the combined Cadet Force. Recently this has met with some resistance, but Meyer is a staunch believer in this, and when necessary some " moral " persuasion is brought to bear. Political opinions are held and tolerated, and many are the arguments around this topic, and fierce. Meyer is of the Establishment, and while he is capable of asking a rich industrialist for the large sum necessary to enable the promising boy of poor parents to come to Millfield (where the fees are considerably higher than those for Eton) or persuading his Governors, as he did not so very long ago, to instal a " Language Laboratory," his views certainly tend towards the right rather than towards the left.

How did Millfield start?

" I was teaching in India, about twenty pupils in one very long room at the top of a palace, ages twenty-three down to three, and I chopped them up into reasonable sorts of divisions, and took them in arithmetic and reading (those who could understand English) . . . we got to know each other, so I got some experience of the tutorial method, different levels of age and ability handled at the same time . . . my main job was to get the small boys into English public schools and the older ones into University and I am glad to say they all managed it . . . imagine doing Latin in a temperature of 120 degrees at the top of a palace, the heat curled the leaves, we must have looked absolutely idiotic, gasping for breath . . . you could have fried an egg on the stone floor where the sun came through the window . . . I had to bring them home to England, to a house that my mother and father had taken for all of us to be, a place where these children could stay in the holidays, a kind of headquarters and we to be the guardians, and that was Millfield! . . . We had only been here about two months when the Maharajah flew in and said it was much too expensive and his State was in a bad way and he had to economize, so please would I pack up. I said fine, but what about a little thing like compensation for loss of salary, arrears of salary etc., a mere £4,500! 'You must write to me about that' he replied (I got £400), so apart from two little boys sent by the Indian Government, paying three guineas each a week, they all went. This was 1935. The upkeep of the house and grounds necessitated employment of seven men—on a total income of six guineas. Somehow we struggled along, the local tradespeople were marvellous, they said they would not send in any bills till I got money to pay them. I wanted to finish with it all, but these people begged me to stay on, and what happened was that another Maharajah, the son of the great Rangit Singhi, asked me to come out and be the Head of the Princes' College in India, but as it would take me six months to move, I had to see if there was anything I could do in the meantime . . . I found that various people needed teaching, the Rector had a couple of children (that would be worth about ten bob a week!) then there were some very difficult nuts that had to be cracked on the teaching side, people who had failed exams, one Squadron Leader's son who was alleged by his father to be absolutely plumb stupid and lazy. I said 'let me have half an hour with him and I'll let you know if he can do what you want' which was for the lad to get into Cambridge. I examined this boy and found his I.Q. to be between 125 and 130 but he was absolutely terrified and dominated by his father who was a very brave man, a war hero. I told this very worthy but difficult man that I would take on his boy and get the boy through his exams provided he stayed away from the boy and did not even demand to see a glimpse of the work until the exams were over. The father agreed, the boy came, and about three weeks later, the father breezed through the door having changed his mind. 'I am not going to put up with you being here. This is my house' I said, and reminded him of his promise . . . the boy stayed and passed all his exams, went to Cambridge and got a perfectly good second in History. I am not anti-discipline or anything like that, but obviously this father-son relationship was a very bad one . . . the parents were so thrilled and grateful that whenever they heard people talking about the difficulties of educating their children, they chipped in and told them to go down to Millfield in Somerset where I would do the job. He brought in droves of boys, so, you see, we survived by succeeding. Some of the early boys were doing shockingly badly at school, but were found to be very teachable, and that's how it all began . . ."

11

The Creatives

TO be gifted creatively, is to be blessed—and yet saddled—
with an inward abundance, a profusion of thought and feeling.
Blessed, by virtue of the depth and variety of responses to life,
and saddled with the confusion that must necessarily exist when
the condition is such that it can be described as an embarrassment
of riches.

The creative mind is responsible, directly or indirectly, for all
that is good and enlightening, and beautiful. The owner of such
a mind has a responsibility and duty to the world. The world
needs what he has, potentially, to offer.

Why, then, should it be so often necessary for genius of a high
creative order to lead to despair and, occasionally, psychosis? Was
it inevitable that Van Gogh should mutilate himself, that Peter
Warlock (Phillip Heseltine) should kill himself? That Marlowe, in
the grip of a self-destructive attraction to the gutter, should be
murdered by one of its inhabitants?

A dancing star can emerge only from chaos—no creative person
who has achieved even a modicum of fulfilment will be able to deny
this. But who are the God-like figures who can take the young and
undeveloped creative mind in hand, as it were, and lead it through
the dark and frightening jungle of inward confusion into the
ordered light of day?

Creative children are puzzled and disturbed by what is within
themselves. It is an understatement to say that they are a problem
to their parents and teachers. More, the very nature of their gifts
is such that the conventional yardsticks of assessment do not apply.
It is no wonder that many, ultimately, creatively talented people,

have a history of scholastic failure. They were, simply, not catered for.

There is no such thing as an I.Q. test for creativity. True enough, it can be used as a predictor, but in which case, who is looking for what? And what, also, is this infinitely flexible, colourful and charged commodity that the educators are trying to measure?

But there are people of insight who are attempting to " place " such children, and interesting although not conclusive work has been done, for instance, at the University of Minnesota. In this particular case, the " field " of investigation was contained by an over-all average of gifted types, so it is not surprising that the level of educative achievement did not vary much from that group who were of high intelligence, and those whose intelligence was high but who were, also, assessed as creative.

What did emerge, however, was the difference in attitude to the acquirement of knowledge, and in his work connected with the results of this research, Professor E. A. Torrance came to the conclusion that the processes by which the creative child reaches *his* conclusions are, concisely (1) preparation (2) incubation (3) illumination and (4) revision.

During the first two processes, the child needs to read, explore the subject in various ways, and then discuss what he has read with the person he has chosen to be his guide. (The element of choice with regard to a mentor is important . . . teacher and pupil have to be on the same " wavelength." The " creative " has no time for those who do not understand him). During the time normally devoted to general discussion, the pupil is analysing what he has learned, testing it out against his knowledge of relevant subjects (and this on a deep level) and then comes the element which can never be measured, the creative flash of insight that carries him far beyond the ordinary reasoning of even the highly intelligent child.

To have such a child in a class would, one might think, inspire in a teacher a sense of thankfulness for his vocation. Unfortunately, the " symptoms " of creativeness are all too easy to confuse, on a superficial level, with the far-away look of day-dreaming that is the mark of the under-achiever, the one whose attention has not been captured, the one who does not seem to want to bother.

How is a teacher to distinguish between the two? How can he be checked from the rude awakening he may be provoked into administering? This, apparent, daydreaming is an emotionally charged process of internal discovery, and the stifling of it is dangerous to mental health, but there is no way of recognizing it as such, at a more superficial level.

The most that one can hope for is that parent or teacher should be aware that they have the problem of dealing with a creative mind, and the least they should do is to attempt to provide the sort of climate needed in which it can develop.

To be creative is to be different, and to be different is to invoke the wrath of Society which, life being what it is, is often provoked into revengefulness because it is up against something it does not understand. It feels even more threatened by the creative person than by the ordinary " egg head " for creatives seem to care little for the rewards of their insight although eager, even longing, for the approval of those they feel might be sympathetic to their particular brand of uniqueness. The rest can go hang. Praise from the " infidels," the *non-cognoscenti,* goes for nothing, and they are not afraid to say as much. " He's too cocky. What's the point in praising him? Let's ignore him . . ." is the natural reaction to child or adult, and the playing down process begins, a reaction in the form of self-defence, and the child is hurt and bewildered.

With the weight of their gift on their shoulders, it is not surprising that creative children have difficulty in making friends, a fact which is often accentuated by emotional retardation. This form of immaturity would seem to go hand in hand with both the creative mind and the mind of high intelligence.

Friends are very important to young " creatives " because they often have a deep-seated feeling of inferiority. Everybody else seems to know about trains and the latest " pop " idol. Not to share a concern with such things, not to be interested in what the " group " is interested in, makes the child feel an outsider. Thus, when such a child does make a friend, it may well be a friend for life. There has to be a shared response on the deepest possible level.

A compensation to make up for the lack of easily found relationships, is the ability to develop a philosophy of life far earlier than most of us do. This could be due to an unusually early awareness of failure, and the need, out of compulsive necessity to complete work in hand, to try again and again to reach a goal which approximates to the original unattainable vision.

Again, there is an additional pitfall in the emotional progress of the creative child, for creativity demands sensitivity (which is a feminine virtue) and, at the same time, independence (a masculine attribute). As a result, creative children sometimes suppress their creativity in the endeavour to conform in the maintenance of their sex rôles, especially if these rôles are given undue weight by parent or teacher, the people above all from whom they need to gain love and approbation.

To cause even further conflict, creative children need to work on their own; they have, to a greater degree than others, the quality of application. Once they have commenced a task, they cannot stop working, and this compulsion, this feeling of " being driven " to complete the task in hand is very marked. When interrupted, they tend to be aggressive and if it happens too often when the children are too young, there is always the danger that they may give up entirely. The future for such a child is bleak, a succession of jobs, never the right one, he complains, and always a sense of melancholy and the vague feeling that something has been lost forever, he knows not what. But this does not mean that a creative child has to be completely overbearing for the good of his health, and rule the entire household, as the following case illustrates:

In the Spring of 1965, the exceptional gifts of a small boy came to the attention of the National Press. From their report, it was learnt that a potential painter of genius was in the making, but what was of greater interest within the context of this book, was the background to the boy's activities.

From the time he was a baby, he had loved to scribble with a pencil, as thousands of toddlers do. He was then given coloured crayons, and, at this point, the mother noticed that, for his age, he had an unusually well developed sense of colour.

So he was given paints, but because an entire household cannot be disrupted by the efforts of one small boy (and also because the wise parents did not want to frustrate him by continually telling him not to make a mess) he was told he could work in the garage when his father's car was not there.

Now, at the age of six, he has just completed a seven foot painting of the local church—a painting not much less than twice his own height! Whether or not this child fulfils his early promise and develops into a painter of genius is beside the point. Indeed, when asked what he would like to be when he grows up, he replies " an astronomer." But there is no doubt that he is highly creative and searching always for new ways of expressing himself. He has the gift, the application, he likes to be left alone to pursue his gift, and he is not afraid of being different. He has been lucky in being the exceptional child of exceptional parents.

But not even the wisest parent can produce a completely satis-factory answer to the problem resulting from the schism between conception and achievement in the case of a creative. No embryo creative genius will ever be able to realize, in actuality, the vision that was in his mind, the poem that he felt, the music that he, inwardly, heard. And this is where an enlightened parent of such a child can be of invaluable assistance—in helping the child to come to terms with his own limitations. For to be aware, even excited, at one's brilliant child, and then to expect too much, can produce in the child a heightened feeling of loneliness, away and above the loneliness that even the most balanced creative mind, no matter how young or how old, is bound to experience continually. To be so aware of one's own uniqueness has this disadvantage, but to be aware also, that the parent one loves and on whom one's happiness depends, does not understand, is a painful and traumatic experi-ence. Such a situation might sharpen the gift, bring to it a new intensity and plant also, the seeds of unbalance and despair so that, like Van Gogh, escape into psychosis might be the only answer, flight from a world which brings only pain.

Creativity refuses to be categorized. It is a law unto itself, and in his study of *A Thousand Gifted Children,* Terman reported sadly, in a follow up, that among them, they had produced not one com-poser of any outstanding merit, not one writer, artist or sculptor. There were some in the groups who showed outstanding talent and became Professors of University Departments in their particular

LEFT: Young Genius.
Yehudi Menuhin
aged seven

BELOW: Gifted young musicians at
the Yehudi Menuhin School

The Young Visiters
or Mr Saltena's plan

by Daisy Ashford

Chap 1
Quite a young girl

Mr Salteena was an elderly
man of 42 and was fond
of asking people to stay
with him. He had quite
a young girl staying with
him of 17 named Ethel
Monticue. Mr Saltena
had dark short hair
and mustache and
wiskers which were very
black and twisty He
was middle sized and he

Photo: Chatto & Windus

First page of *The Young Visiters* written at the age
of nine by Daisy Ashford

Daisy Ashford—self-confident nine-years-old author

Girls and boys write and produce
their own newspaper

subjects, but creative genius is a very rare bird indeed, and does its best to evade the researcher.

Indeed, very few child prodigies show the same amount of talent in later life, although the field of music seems to include the exceptions. Both Mozart and Yehudi Menuhin were child prodigies whose early days bear many points of similarity, the long tours from city to city, the admiration of the crowds, performing at concerts to the point of exhaustion and then, instead of being allowed to rest, having to be polite to people who might turn out to be patrons. Some inner resource of integrity and toughness must exist to make it possible for these children to survive a world which is hungry for their divine gift and seems prepared, at the same time, to swallow them in a spasm of greed. To be a genius has, indeed, its disadvantages!

In general, the creative child's development tends to be uneven. This may be due to the need for the incubation period during which period, development tends to slow down on the top, but a great deal is going on below. It is during this time, which may be prolonged, that the child may come into conflict with his family, for if his creative ability has been recognized, the tendency is to push him. Such an attempt to make genius run, while it is in the process of finding its feet, can do much harm. Uniquely gifted children are easily exploited (especially by their parents, either consciously or unconsciously), but the importance of a foundation of good mental and physical health before the age of five cannot be too strongly emphasized. The strain to which the creative artist will be subjected throughout his life will be prodigious, and a good foundation may well save him from breakdown. Creative people, as a race, seem to have little sense of self-preservation, so it is up to those around them, when they are very young, to give them opportunity for expression and, at the same time, persuade them to take their place in the family circle with the ordinary obligations and responsibilities that this implies. Thus, a foundation of stability is consolidated.

The truly creative child will have a wide range of activities and interests, although, perhaps, it is only in the case of Leonardo da Vinci that such a variety of early interests persisted into later life.

Good Nursery Schools can provide a real outlet for the creative and high I.Q. child from cramped surroundings. Here, for perhaps the first time, he is able to play with sand and water, to experiment with new material without the fear of being reproached for untidiness. As a result, his fantasy-play can occur over a longer period, until he is ready to pass onto something else. Gradually, the indiscriminate indulgence of interests will be refined, will narrow and deepen until the basic core of creativity is reached, and the child and his gift are one.

The time will come, perhaps, when an enlightened world will quickly recognize the potential genius amongst us, and provide, liberally, the sort of institutions that are best suited to develop unique gifts. At the moment, it is only the *exceptionally lucky* gifted child who finds himself in a milieu in which his sensitive talent can be nutured to its greatest advantage. Two such institutions have been visited by the authors, and both are models of their kind, and respected throughout the artistic world.

THE ROYAL BALLET SCHOOL

Dancing is, at once, the most primitive and one of the most complex of the arts. From the dawn of human life, Man has expressed every emotion he feels through the Dance, even in the most indirect manner. A child, nowadays, sent to a " Saturday Dancing Class " may well be indirectly benefiting (if he is able to!) from an upgrade in his parent's financial status. On an anthropological level, it is no coincidence that the boy, or girl, should be sent to learn how to dance shortly after his parents have experienced the joy of increased material prosperity. Several thousand years ago *they* would have done the dancing—and, of course, they still might do so in the course of an impulsive and celebratory " splash " in the form of a dinner-dance.

But a primitive urge to dance, as a form of self-expression, and the classical refinements which take such an activity into the higher realms of enduring art, can hardly be equated. Yet it was not until 1947 that England could boast an institution worthy of instruction in this wholly important and satisfying art form, an institution which could spot, quickly, the seeds of exceptional talent in people young enough to be moulded, as they necessarily have to be, by many years of rigorous training, in the pursuit of acquiring all-important technique.

Pure art transcends all national boundaries, and is, at the same time, a reflection of the land from where it springs. Between the two World Wars, Dame Ninette de Valois realized that the slavish copying of the Russians, who had led the world of classical ballet for so long, was not the answer to the establishment of an English tradition of classical dance. The formation of a National Ballet Company was one thing, but a Company with its own inimitable style was another.

She founded the Sadler's Wells School in 1931, and the selected pupils used to turn up at the Theatre after their day's work at a conventional school. This was, of course, an impossible strain on the children, an addition to the normal strain of learning and home-work; in the form of rush-hour travel and physically exhausting exercises. But it took another sixteen years before the ideal solution presented itself in the form of a Ballet School which, within its framework of tuition, also incorporated the facilities for conventional education of Grammar School standard.

At first the School occupied premises which were not large enough to include living quarters. Then, in 1955, it was made possible to take over the White Lodge, in Richmond Park. This classically beautiful Palladian edifice, built originally as a hunting lodge for George I in 1727, and used by Royalty until 1922, placed as it is amidst the gracious formality of its Park, could not be more ideally situated. Much of the original interior is still preserved, but classrooms have now replaced the adjacent stables, and the Anna Pavlova Memorial Studio was built out of funds donated by her husband, to be a tribute to one of the greatest dancers of our time.

As one enters the inner hall, with its fine curved staircase, it is not the many cases containing original documents nor the many exquisite glass-cased porcelain effigies of dancers that hold the eye, but a feeling of light. Light is everywhere, even on the darkest Winter's day, streaming in through the multitude of long windows, reflecting off the gleaming white paint. So in accordance with the lightness of step of the child pupils, moving with gaiety about their various tasks, living in an atmosphere which is utterly conducive to their gifts, their deepest needs.

To be a pupil of the Royal Ballet School involves certain important conditions. A dancer's instrument is his own body. There is no external aid, no mellow Stradivarius to play on, no grained marble to chisel. Nothing but the human body, so, in the process of selection, certain physical characteristics are essential. Girls are taken on between the ages of ten and eleven. Boys have to be a year older, slightly taller and strongly built, as, in addition to their solo work, they have to be able to lift a female partner with ease in the process, sometimes, of a complex series of dance steps. Both boys and girls must have straight backs, well-shaped legs, well-proportioned heads set on strong shoulders, and not be too heavily built. This may sound like a counsel of perfection, but small faults can be, and are, corrected as the training proceeds. The one important bugbear, that of becoming too tall while training (girls must not grow taller than 5ft. 6in. and boys a little more), has largely been eliminated by the examination that they receive at Great Ormond Street Hospital where a famous orthopaedic surgeon can gauge eventual growth to within an inch and a half.

Having been assessed as physically right to be taken on, the pupil then has to satisfy the formal educative demands of the School. They have to be highly intelligent (and, indeed, are given an I.Q. test) for the simple yet practical reason that, unfortunately, there is no guarantee that burning desire plus early promise adds up to a dancer. They must have, also, the basic training for alternative careers. Indeed, as occasionally happens, a pupil makes the initial move in asking to be released from the School and, having kept up with his conventional academic training, has thus been enabled to fit into a sixth form at some other school where a different career is decided upon as far away from ballet as, for instance, engineering!

Thus, the physical test and the intelligence test have been passed, and the pupil is installed.

For all the fact that the initial contract is for only one year—a year of probation—the School staff have to be satisfied, during the audition, with the child's co-ordination and ease of movement, and his general attitude towards the severe discipline that he has to impose upon himself for all the eight years of training, this in addition to the intelligence (with the concomitants of quick thinking and a keen mind) that is essential to exploit the sheerly bodily gifts to the full.

The academic work at White Lodge is in the eminently capable and sympathetic hands of Lady Agnew, M.A., who tutored at the Universities of Edinburgh and Hamilton (Canada) before joining the Royal Ballet School. This remarkable woman has warmth of manner and enthusiasm, not only for her immediate scholastic concern, but for the artistic ambitions of her pupils, an enthusiasm that is of prime importance where the comparatively mundane attractions of orthodox schooling can easily be considered as no more than a trial compared to the basic desire to be a dancer.

All the pupils, boys and girls, are required to take five to nine subjects at " O " level and parents, occasionally, express their alarm at such an apparently exhausting task—the amount of academic work *plus* the arduous training necessary in early days to prepare the developing dancer for the far more complex routine of later studies. If there need be an explanation for what might seem an unduly hard life for a child, perhaps it is that these children are, in fact, super-normal. Also, and this is important, they are surrounded by every facility to make their task no more energy consuming than necessary, no travelling at all, for instance.

Round about the age of sixteen, the pupils leave White Lodge for premises closer to the centre of London, where, also, a few take their studies into "A" level standards. But, by this time, dancing and allied subjects occupy most of their working time.

Throughout the long training period, the pupils are given every opportunity to keep in close contact with their homes, to which they return during " normal " school holidays. Even those from as far away as Ghana (with expenses paid for by a private benefactor) are flown home once a year. But all the while (where possible) there is the closest contact between the staff of the School and the parents of the pupils, enabling problems to be discussed as they occur, *if* they occur. In the case of such highly gifted children, team work on the part of all who have their interests at heart is essential.

There is, also, constant and close liaison between academic and dancing staff, and each child's academic progress is continually under review. Teachers of the ordinary school subjects may not, even, be particularly interested in ballet, but were chosen because they were known to be good teachers who, above all, were interested in the teaching of unusually gifted children in an unconventional setting.

Needless to say, the self-imposed discipline of the young dancer stands him in good stead when he is concerned with the prosaic, but important, classroom duties. But far from evincing sobriety and a seriousness of conduct, the young dancer skates through his work with aplomb, living and working, as he does, in an atmosphere he loves. Boys and girls alike, at the School, often bubble over with the sheer joy of their life.

Unlike their Russian equivalents, the juniors at the Royal Ballet School do not dance with the Company, although sometimes they participate in an annual matinee performance given at the Royal Opera House, so their school work, at whatever level, is never interrupted, this, even when they are transferred to the Senior School, for it is obligatory for all boys and girls under the age of $17\frac{1}{2}$ to attend classes in English, French, history of art, ballet and other allied subjects. Naturally, music plays an overwhelmingly important part in the life of a dancer, and the older children at White Lodge attend concert rehearsals at the Royal Festival Hall. But all in all, the basic difference between the education of these young dancers and most young scholars of their age, is in the realm of sport. The girls are not taught hockey, lacrosse or even cricket (as is the case in some public schools for girls) while the boys seem to prefer swimming and fencing. Nothing won on the playing fields of Eton will ever be of much account in the thinking of those connected with the Royal Ballet School!

There are one or two problems, the most constant of which, not unnaturally, is finance. The number of local authorities prepared to meet the fees of the School grows yearly, especially now that a conventional Grammar School education is incorporated in the prospectus. But equipment (clothes, pumps, etc.) are not covered by such grants, and the students have to find the money for such items themselves. Another problem is the low numbers of male student dancers, for when the balance lies heavily on the number of girls, it is difficult to plan a genuinely co-educational system.

Gradually, thanks to the remarkable pioneering work of Dame Ninette de Valois, the almost non-existent status of the male dancer in this country is changing, and the gifted young dancer will one day be a figure of national pride. Thus, as the years go by, it will become less and less necessary to import foreign dancers to provide the important " star quality " executants so necessary to keep up the glamour of the art of dancing.

THE YEHUDI MENUHIN SCHOOL

When his children were very small, Yehudi Menuhin used to take them to their Highgate home by bus. They were born into music, their father was famous and lionized, they mixed with great artists and lived amidst beautiful surroundings. But this does not constitute life. Their father wished them to look about them, see how other people, less fortunate than themselves, lived, to study the poor dwellings that flanked the approaches to his own pleasant district, to be aware of the " common man " always. It is amazing how much there is to be seen from the top of a bus—if you know what you are looking for!

Humility is an integral part of creative greatness. The belief that one's gift has been given to benefit the world is a continual incentive to deepen and expand the gift, so that the world shall experience ever greater delight. But this philosophical attitude is still dependent upon the sheer ability to improve, the ability to have absorbed, early on, the necessary techniques that make it all possible.

This means hard work and, from a very early age, the gifted child musician has to undergo a rigorous training in basic dexterity —yet he still has to be a child, with allowances made for his childish needs, if he is to develop into an emotionally secure and integrated adult.

To be allowed to be a child, yet trained to be an artist, involves a sensitivity on the part of the teacher that in itself amounts to a gift. The selection of such teachers, the availability of premises conducive to such training where, at the same time, the young peformer can be concerned with worldly and practical matters, these have been the aims of Yehudi Menuhin for many years. It was in 1963 that he was enabled to put this aim into concrete form, when he founded his now famous School.

There were, to begin with, some half a dozen trustees and fifteen potential pupils, aged from nine to thirteen. The idea was to give the pupils the best possible musical education, by finding the best teachers for them, establishing them in London, and also organizing their general education. At first, these fifteen were placed in a Kensington hostel, and attended to their academic studies at the A.E.T. But this was not satisfactory because the conditions under which the pupils lived were very restricted. The hostel had no " special " rooms for their study and practice and the teachers were forced to visit them there; there were no facilities for playing out of doors, nothing but the parks, and they had to spend too much time getting to school. Somewhere had to be found where orthodox schooling and music training could be accomplished under the same roof. Ultimately, the present building was found, and the work of starting up a school for music began in earnest.

The building which now houses the School was built about a hundred years ago, and is some twenty-five miles from London. Once a management training centre for an industrial concern, it is comfortably organized with central heating and fitted carpets everywhere, with more of the feeling of the study than the schoolroom about it. Behind the School is a stable block and beside this a pair of well constructed white-painted prefabs, each of them a classroom. And around it all is fifteen acres of garden, the home of many birds, and for much of the year the air is filled with bird song.

Here, as at the Royal Ballet School, the children move about purposefully, talk well to strangers (and there is a constant stream of visitors to this pioneer venture) but as in a Château town in France —friendly to the tourists—one gets the impression that with sunset and the departure of all strangers, the real life and purpose of the place emerges.

It is here that so many children are given a first chance to develop their talent for music, but it is always taken into account that a precocious and promising start is no indication of staying power and application. To be a concert artist far more than musical ability is needed. There needs to be an emotional foundation as impregnable as rock, yet as sensitive as the filament of a lamp.

Shortly before the Summer of 1964, M. Gazelle had been appointed as Music Principal. He, in fact, has a professional commitment at the Conservatoire of Ghent so (1965) has to spend half of his working week in Belgium, and half in England. But half of a rare man is better than the whole of one less accomplished, and it is M. Gazelle who is responsible for the selection of pupils and teachers. He also teaches the piano.

So much for the sheerly musical side. But what about the academic education of these most talented youngsters? It was thought that the man who should be in charge of this important aspect, the man really who was more concerned with the child than the budding musician, would himself have to be sympathetic to the aims of the school without necessarily being a professional musician. An exclusive devotion to music in such a man would, wisely, have been regarded as suspect, as this was not the element of the child that was to be his concern.

Such a man as was required arrived in the presence of Anthony Brackenbury, a tall, quiet, kindly man, an amateur performer himself and also an appreciator of good music. About him is all the calmness and stability that is needed in the orthodox education of children who are, basically, involved in a pursuit that is both arduous and highly emotional.

Lessons are, of course, programmed so as not to interfere with the musical training, but a certain purposefulness on the part of the young pupils (they all know what they want to be) permeates their attitude to the purely academic work. Taking, as it does, so many forms, music has far less potential frustration in its employ than other arts. A child might discover that an early flair for piano playing did not develop, although his interpretative gifts are such that he might easily turn into a unique conductor. Then again, at the other end of the scale, a developing bent towards the academic side might result in a period, ultimately, at some University, and later an appointment in the capacity of musicologist.

Music is a great avenue of escape from emotional problems. A musical child with a difficult, even hurt, temperament, can sublimate to an extraordinary degree, and obtain a level of contentment throughout life which would be denied another child without such a means of escape.

But, on the whole, the pupils of the Menuhin School present a remarkably " normal " face to the world. All highly gifted children are up against unusual parental problems, especially as parents see a second chance for themselves in their children. Thus, there is the tendency to " live through the child " and wish it to accomplish all that the parent was unable to achieve, an attitude that is fraught with danger and the likelihood of pushing the pupil into illness and breakdown.

Brackenbury is very much aware of this danger. For all the fact that the pupils are given every oportunity to be in constant touch with absent parents—even to the extent of a kiosk telephone exclusively for their use—the parents are discouraged from giving way to over-anxious concern which would be ruinous to the child's healthy emotional development. If they are so inclined, such parents have to try to keep *their* problem at home.

Bearing in mind that there are so many ways of earning a living as a musician, here there is less emphasis placed on academic achievement than, for instance, in the Royal Ballet School. Less attention is paid to measured intelligence, although intelligence has to be high to begin with, otherwise the child would not be able to master the many adjustments that have to be made before proficiency is attained. Selection is on the strength of sheer musicality, accomplished as much by intuition as by scientific testing. Musicians do, above all, tend to be people of intuition.

At the School, too, is an emphasis on external peace, the peace of sympathetic surroundings in a beautiful setting, a necessary peace to compensate for the inner turbulence of such children. Indeed, the children seem to be gay, hard working and confident.

For the most part, Local Authorities are willing to pay the fees for the children selected. Some music teachers would like to explore the possibility of dealing with pupils as young as five. But this involves the additional problems of finding teachers equipped to deal with those of such tender years, and what also has to be taken into account are the emotional problems that separation from parents, in the case of children so young, creates.

Yet, a gift for music, if given fertile ground to develop, seems to take care of such problems, to a large extent, and the time will surely come when there will be no such thing as an exceptional and, at the same time, unrecognized gift for music. In the meantime, Yehudi Menuhin is giving those lucky ones in his charge, the ones who are being catered for as they should be catered for, the chance of a lifetime.

12

Some Short Cuts to Achievement

"THERE was a young lady who swallowed a horse—she died of course!" In the original of this popular children's rhyme it was an old lady who swallowed the horse, but one of Dickens' young ladies, on revealing her miserable inability to define such a creature had to swallow this factual description: "Quadruped. Gramnivorous. Forty teeth, namely twenty-four grinders, four eye teeth and twelve incisive. Sheds coat in Spring, in marshy countries sheds hoofs too . . ."

No-one is yet on record of having physically choked to death on facts, and neither is mental asphyxia one of the more common diseases of childhood because an indigestible conglomeration of facts is rejected by children in the same way as undigested food is regurgitated by a baby. Nobody can be forced to acquire knowledge, even when it is considered essential that they do.

"Now, what I want is facts," said Mr Gradgrind (*Dombey and Son*). "I teach these boys and girls nothing but facts. Facts alone are wanted in life. Plant nothing else . . ." But there are now ways of planting facts in which they are made so interesting that their acquirement can amount to an "adventure" in knowledge, an essential heightening, especially in the field of teaching the gifted whose need for "facts" is far ahead of their ability to understand the mechanics of the facts in question.

At a later age, of course, when there is a more detached interest in acquiring necessary knowledge, there is no need to dress up facts in coats of many colours, but a child is still a child even when he is brilliant, and unable to overcome an instinctive rejection of that which is not palatable.

There is, incidentally, an important and concomitant advantage with regard to facilitating the acquirement of knowledge by gifted children. They have the opportunity, when amongst those less gifted, to pass on their knowledge in such a way that they are enabled to develop towards a healthy realization of their own usefulness, in a social sense. Thus the tendency towards the feeling of isolation, so often the big drawback in the otherwise rich mental life of the high I.Q. child, does not take precedence and the ability to adjust to " group " feeling is enhanced. This may be no more than identification with a teacher, passing on to his contemporaries what he has acquired from his own instruction, but in a non-didactic way.

Perhaps the most important innovation in the field of instructing the very young and gifted child is the use of the Initial Teaching Alphabet. Naturally this innovation is a help to all children, gifted or not, but for a truly gifted child the importance of being able to read and spell words which, by virtue of the quirky spelling of the English language, are usually beyond his grasp, cannot be over-estimated.

For all children, and for the gifted child in particular, learning to read is one of the most important things that ever happens to him. It opens so many doors, and provides him with an independence of thought that very few other things which he will learn during the rest of his life will give him.

Sir Cyril Burt says with authority that " reading is by far the most important subject a young child learns at school. It is also the most difficult to teach. English in its orthography is more erratic and irregular than any other contemporary language; that is the price one pays for its composite origin, a feature to which so much of its richness and flexibility is due."

One of the most quickly noticeable attributes of gifted children is their delight in solving problems, how fascinated they are by them and the ease with which they seem to be able to deal with them. The exponents of the teaching of reading by means of the Initial Teaching Alphabet (or I.T.A. as it is now generally known) would say that the method was of special use to the gifted child because it posed the very kind of problems that he would enjoy solving.

The I.T.A. is, in fact, a two stage approach to reading. It was evolved by Sir James Pitman from the original designs made by Sir Isaac Pitman and his collaborator, A. J. Ellis. The actual type in which they are printed was designed by C. N. Fellows and D. H. J. Schenck, who are well-known consultant typographers, to fit the scheme which is based on our ordinary Roman lower case alphabet leaving out, therefore, all capital letters and omitting *q* and *x* altogether, and adding twenty other characters, each with its own sound, some of which are based on ordinary diagraphs, but others completely new.

The idea behind the method is concerned with the attempt to overcome confusion caused by the different ways actual letters are written in lower case, in capitals and in cursive (joined up writing) and also by the different ways the words are sounded although they seem to be spelled more or less alike—*through, thorough, trough*—or when they look different but are pronounced the same—*zoo, two, flew, shoe.*

In 1960 research began at the Institute of Education (London University) and a committee of linguists and educationalists was appointed. These included Professor Cyril Burt and Sir James Pitman. Later that same year John Downing, a Senior Lecturer in Educational Psychology, was appointed to make inquiries as to how this method could be used in schools and to help in the choosing of readers that could be transliteralized into I.T.A., for with the new alphabet new type had been devised. Education authorities were asked for their support and the scheme had the blessing of the Ministry of Education. Meetings of Head Teachers were called and the experiment got under way in a surprisingly short time, first in Infant schools. Twenty-one schools took part originally, and by September 1963 this number had been extended to two hundred-and-thirty-three schools and some ninety-four Junior, Secondary and Special schools, and also remedial centres.

In the process of communication, learning to write is as important as learning to read. The child who learns to read by I.T.A. must also learn to write by it, and from the reports so far received this does not seem to have presented undue difficulty, except that certain parents feel excluded from an " area " of their children inasmuch as they cannot understand what their child is writing! Parent-teacher Association meetings are, in fact, held at the schools using this method and those parents who are interested enough to attend are encouraged to buy cheap story books in I.T.A. script so that the children can read at home and even share their new task with their parents.

The most common fear expressed by teachers at the original meetings was that I.T.A. would have a bad effect on the children's spelling in general but, judging by the low standard obtaining in many places currently, nothing was likely to make it worse, and almost any change must inevitably be for the better. The fact that spelling, when first learned by the children, follows phonetic principles is, the sponsors claim, an advantage because having mastered this and had freedom of expression, when the time comes for the changeover to ordinary script, the child can be introduced to the mysteries of English spelling as a separate and intriguing problem, but not at the time when the child's capacity has to be employed to the full to achieve the very preliminaries of reading and writing, and as the changeover is one reached by each individual child at his own pace, there would seem to be no problem in acquiring orthodox spelling.

The fact that problem solving and the joy in doing so is part of the gifted child's pattern may, it is hoped, be furthered by the use of I.T.A. For instance, W. B. Dockerell, as educational psychologist, points out that the development of intelligence is influenced by childhood experiences and in the home where there are few books and the parents have a limited vocabulary, the child is handicapped until he has learned to read for himself. If we help him to accelerate this process, we are doing him a great favour and setting him free to make use of his gifts, perhaps for the first time.

The headmistress of an Infant School in South East Anglia has in her charge a considerable number of gifted children, and finds there is often a gap between the child's technical skill and his comprehension in reading. Also, the knowledge of life they acquire by their heightened perception is in great contrast to the dull stuff given them in the reading books considered suitable for their chronological age at school. In this way they quickly become bored and run the risk of becoming under-achievers.

In this school, therefore, an enlightened headmistress has made it possible for very young, but gifted, children to have done much reading even before going to their Junior School at the age of seven. When asked her opinion of the possible difficulty the gifted child had when the time came for him to change over from the I.T.A. script to the ordinary script, she related the following: " John was reading to me a story he liked from his I.T.A. copy. I had beside me a book containing the ordinary version of the same story. At one point I gave him the other book and asked him to find the same story and read this out to me. This he did without the slightest difficulty and when we reached the bottom of the page, we changed back again and he continued without a pause. John was six at the time with an I.Q. of about 140 and his only comment at the end of the lesson was that *his* book was cleaner than *mine*!"

Writing does not seem to present any difficulties either, and children get an enormous amount of pleasure out of their journals. They are not held back when they first begin by the difficulties of spelling and so are able to express their ideas far more freely. Their spoken language is richer too because of the amount of reading they have been able to do. " We were preparing a Christmas programme and a small girl of not yet six years was to act as Chairman. I said to her ' I think that at this time I ought to speak to our visitors,' to which she replied ' That's quite all right, I will do it for you. I can extemporize for a few minutes.' That is an example of confident comprehension and pleasure in words."

There is no doubt that the gifted four or five year old is tempted to use his technical skill on matters beyond his comprehension, and the experimental work now in hand employing the use of the I.T.A. may prove, in the not too distant future, that a means of communication has been devised which is truly a short cut to achievement.

Another important and imaginative breakthrough in the teaching of the young and gifted is in the field of mathematics. We must emphasize again that these modern teaching methods are equally

Photo: Henk Snoek

New-style university—Brunel College of Advanced Technology

Children at a monastery intrigued by decorated Easter eggs sent
by the Pope

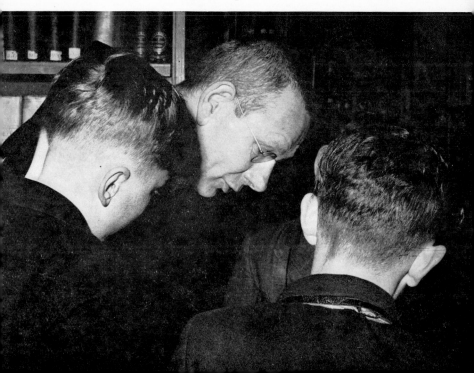

Photo: The Sun

ƚhis iꭓ printed in ƚhe iniſhial teⅽɧiŋ alfabet (i.t.a.) deꭓiend bie ꭓir jæmꭓ pitman. sⲱn aull ɕhildren will lern tⲱ reed and riet ƚhrⲱ ƚhis nue meedium, becauꭓ it iꭓ nou acsepted ƚhat our tradiſhonal alfabet and spelliŋꭓ hav been mœst difficult for ƚhe yuŋ beginner, and ƚhe cauꭓ ov tⲱ slœ progress, and ov muɕh fæluer.

ƚhœꭓ uest tⲱ ƚhe œld wæ mæ fiend it hard tⲱ beleev, but it iꭓ trⲱ, ƚhat ƚhaŋks tⲱ i.t.a. ƚhe very yuŋ beginner lernꭓ tⲱ reed and riet muɕh mor eeꭓily, and cumꭓ very muɕh sⲱner tⲱ enjoi reediŋ and rietiŋ: hee ƚhen (surprieꭓiŋly, wiƚhout effort!), transferꭓ aull ƚhat noledʒ, enjoiment and sucsess tⲱ reediŋ and rietiŋ in our convenſhonal caracterꭓ and spelliŋꭓ œnly.

ƚhis iꭓ ƚhe beginniŋ ov a mœst eksietiŋ bræk-ƚhrⲱ— wiƚh eduecæſhonal and sœſhial implicæſhonꭓ ov græt importanꭓ, ƚhrⲱout ƚhe hœl iŋgliſh speekiŋ wurld.

useful to both the gifted and the child of average intelligence, but it is the gifted who will benefit most, and be enabled to leap ahead in their development and not be hampered by obstacles in the realms of, for instance, the abstract.

Numbers as such are abstract, and the ability to grasp their function and use this knowledge to practical ends implies an ability for abstract thought. If you tell a child that twice 2 is 4 he will learn this parrot-fashion when he has had it drummed into his head enough times, rather like learning a simple piece of poetry without knowing what it means. How much easier for him to lay down two lots of two pencils so that he can appreciate beyond doubt that twice two pencils are four pencils. This simple illustration is, basically, an example of the thinking behind the new conception of teaching mathematics to the young, and will be seen as relating the abstract to the concrete. And the opposite similarly applies—two lots of two pencils equals four? Right, let us remove these pencils and deal now with the abstract symbol, the figure 2. If twice two pencils (or rubbers, or teddybears) equals four pencils, rubbers or teddybears, then twice 2 must be 4.

To the very young the use of the concrete in learning mathematics is to make an adventure of an otherwise colourless occupation. Very high intelligence does not necessarily imply a penchant for abstract thinking. One of the most brilliant children of all time was Margery Fleming who died in her eighth year, was a friend of Sir Walter Scott and kept day-to-day Journals in order that she could marshal her thoughts, for hardly anyone around her could appreciate the ideas of this extraordinary little girl. " I am now going to tell you the horrible and wretched plaege (sic) that my multiplication table gives me. The most devilish thing is eight times eight and seven times seven. It is what Nature herself can't endure," wrote Margery. If she had been alive today, she would have been enabled to get some pleasure out of that " plaege " making multiplication table.

One headmaster at least has found that even the use of an object as unexciting as a counter can be of tremendous help, and this particular man is greatly in favour of the abacus (a calculating frame with balls sliding on wires) through the use of which many children can solve otherwise—to them—insoluble problems. It is interesting

5

that such a plaything as the abacus has been given to children for thousands of years, yet it is only today that its use in the very fundamentals of learning has been fully appreciated!

It is probably true to say that a real and constructive grasp of mathematics can only begin when the basic concept of numbers has been absorbed, and experimentation has now proved that an early grasp of this concept can, generally speaking, only occur when there has been constant comparison between abstract and concrete. The comparisons can be innumerable and in the very process of comparing, a child's imaginative powers are given the opportunity to be extended to his capacity.

The meaning of " which of you by taking thought can add one cubit to his stature," is not easy to grasp by a Primary School child, but then he can be shown that a cubit extends from elbow to finger-tip, and that a simple measurement is, therefore, related to philosophical thought. Twice 2 is 4 but you can't grow taller by merely thinking about it. On the same level is the problem of measurement by the human foot. Here is a piece of cloth which is as long as four times the length of your foot (walk along it and you will see that this is so). Now, if your friend, whose feet are larger, sells it for a penny a foot, and uses *his* feet as the measure, you will see how it is that he will earn less than if *you* had sold it, using *your* foot as the measure. Thus, elasticity of thought is encouraged, far removed from the rigid learning, parrot-fashion, of tables and measurements, and at the same time the need for standardization is genuinely appreciated. After all, the width of the school corridor does not alter just because you can lie across it with your feet touching one wall and your head the other, while your larger friend has to bend his knees in the same process.

Standardization itself can be made the subject for lively discussion. From the Bible a child will learn that Noah's Ark was so many cubits long and so many cubits high, but when they translate this into modern measurement, they find that the Ark must have been almost as long as the Mersey Tunnel and certainly higher than the local Town Hall! So, decides the child, the Biblical cubit does not seem to be based on a standardized measurement. In the school referred to above, interest in measurement became such that a group of children measured the site of the school and then started to work out whether their school complied with the Ministry of Education specifications relating to the number of children permissible in the building (whose size depended on the area of the site it occupied). Luckily the ruling had not been broken, which is more than can be said for a great many over-crowded schools functioning today. A creative interest in mathematics can reflect negatively on those who promote it!

Just as we have seen how mathematics can be linked with religious knowledge, it can be linked similarly with history, and the intelligent child with access to a library can make his own discoveries. He can discover the ingenious—he can even employ some mechanical aptitude and make a candle clock for himself after having looked it up under " clocks." He might find out about the monk who made a dangerous journey to Spain to get from the Moors the secret of the zero or cypher, prior to the knowledge of which calculation had been so inaccurate.

This continual process of investigating the ramifications of measurements appeals to the gifted child, especially to one in the group of the technically gifted, for members of this group are particularly anxious to translate abstract thought into concrete results. Such a child will delight in making a pendulum and then working out by graphs the time of its swing and the relationship between this and the length of the string from which it hangs. Already at the age of ten the gifted child is continually trying to think out quicker and better ways of arriving at answers. This, naturally, can amount to a challenge and stimulus to his teacher.

Due to such early stimulus in the field of mathematics the child's mind is free to expand into, for instance, the field of co-ordinate geometry, which is often not taught until the Sixth form. These children, with their special ability to see the relationship between one thing and another, are excited by parabolas, circles and elipses, an excitement which is intensified when they read newspaper reports of space exploration. How different from a few years ago when Sixth formers were taught these facts as formulas which they were expected to memorize and which seemed as interesting as a suet pudding and nowhere near as palatable!

It is impossible to calculate how many gifted children may have been lost as mathematicians and scientists by the very fact that the teaching in these subjects in the past was so dull. Nowadays, eight year olds are hanging over the bannisters with home-made pendulums, while others stand below with stop watches. The measurements may not be particularly accurate but mathematics is coming alive and numbers are jumping off the page. Problems should never be divorced from reality (a bath has two outlets and one tap, etc.) and filling exercise books with the answers to such problems is no longer needed. What is the use, in this age of adding machines and computers, of making children multiply 9684573 by 8975, something they will never have to do, in reality, without mechanical aid?

It is in the Teacher Training Colleges that the revolution in the teaching of mathematics is seen at its most urgent. If the gifted child is to be a challenge and not a threat, the teacher must himself be trained in modern methods, so that he can work with rather than against the child. A principal lecturer in mathematics at one such college believes that class teaching as such is disappearing, at least so far as her subject is concerned, and that the sharp edges of subject knowledge are becoming blurred. For example, in measuring surfaces leaves are used and then children can see why the surface area of the leaf (water catchment area) matters to the tree itself. Thus knowledge in a branch of nature study is gained from a lesson in mathematics, and when it is remembered that the gifted are anxious to pass on their discoveries, it will be realized just how important these new methods are.

Four blocks make a cube—a relationship is learned—space and pattern appreciated—the knowledge of angles, squares and equilateral triangles can be used in the design of a tile pattern for a floor—maths, dull old maths, is a thing of the past because twice two astronauts equals four astronauts.

At the age of eleven, Robert D. failed his common entrance examination. Four years later he left school to begin work. He had managed to get through his schooling without passing one single examination. " You've hardly got the brains to be an errand boy," his headmaster had said.

Robert became a trade apprentice. His firm's Education Officer didn't think much of his chances, but allowed him to take time off for attendance at the Kingsway Technical School (London). There he sat for his City and Guilds examination which he managed to scrape through. He had refused to give up because if no-one else believed in him, Robert believed in himself. He transferred to a nearby Technical College, and it was there that he found a teacher who also believed in him.

In quick succession Robert obtained his Ordinary National Certificate in electrical and mechanical engineering, and then took his Higher National Certificate in five subjects. Shortly afterwards he began an automation project which lasted twelve months. This, ultimately, brought him his Technical Diploma. At the age of twenty-two, just to prove he was now capable of it, he took his G.C.E. " O " level in English and, at the time of writing, is to take his "A" level in Mathematics. Robert is twenty-three years old and one of the youngest senior computer analysts in the country.

There are many gifted people like Robert who would seem to be, when they are young, ineducable. Yet if attention had been paid to the verdict of his headmaster or, worse, if so much criticism resulting from his lamentable scholastic record had weakened his belief in himself, a singularly gifted technologist would have been lost to the world, and a singularly unhappy man would be wandering around, the victim, paradoxically, of his own unusual and unrecognized gifts.

The child who is brilliant, but whose mentality is unsuited to academic study, should no longer be left out on a limb. Unfortunately he often is, and many technological jobs are available only to those who, it would appear, possess the magical powers that the achievement of a conventional academic degree would seem to confer on them. The time for a great re-appraisal of ability, on the part of employers, is long overdue, but today it is a College of Advanced Technology which can provide that " short cut to achievement " to a boy or girl whose mentality is such that formal academic training does little for them.

Colleges of Technology are a comparatively recent innovation, and the first one did not start functioning until early in this century. Even so, it was not until the early '30s that, thanks to the pioneer work of Cyril Burt, the very institutions that, one would have thought, were likely to pay more attention to a youngster's technological bent, started to disregard conventional academic prowess. Until then, failure in, for instance, arithmetic meant failing the entrance examination.

This faulty method of selection, plus the fact that until the years after the Second World War there were very few of these colleges, resulted in a considerable population of technologically gifted youngsters being overlooked. It was, however, during the war years that the great re-think occurred. Unfortunately the need for a re-assessment of educative possibilities arose out of the need for an ever-increasing amount of machines made to destroy. It is sad to consider that the awareness, at last, of the need to search for brilliance in our own young people, arose from a need to invent machines that might, one day, be responsible for destroying their creators.

Nevertheless, as a result of the 1944 act, administrators decided to divide Secondary Schools into Secondary Modern, Technical and Grammar Schools, and still there was the feeling of stigma attached to Technical Schools. Irrespective of their bent, children of high intelligence were automatically sent to Grammar Schools, and only those who were patently unable to rise to Grammar School standards found themselves in Technical Schools if their interests seemed to centre round subjects the Colleges were teaching. There was a great wastage of potential technological achievement among certain of the highly intelligent who, condemned as it were to the wrong educative environment, evinced none of their very special and vitally important aptitudes. The result of such wastage can hardly be assessed. But the breakthrough has occurred. Certain Colleges for Advanced Technology will be assuming the status of Technical Universities, and until very recently, this in itself would have seemed a contradiction in terms. Yet it is in the practical atmosphere of these new Universities that the growing breed of gifted technologists will develop and prosper. It is here that their now sought-after gifts will be given the opportunity to flourish into practical achievement.

Some of the tuition available at these institutions is surprising in its ramifications. But let us, at first, consider the more usual set-up in which a gifted young potential engineer found himself. Traditionally, a young student entered university where he stayed for three years, and during which time he received no practical training at all. Even during the long periods of vacation, should he be from a family which was not well-upholstered financially, he would be obliged to seek the sort of casual employment which is geared to people of no qualifications whatsoever, working late shift in an ice-cream factory, sorting letters at the Post Office during the Christmas deluge, or even out-and-out labouring on building sites.

Nobody is criticising such worthy activity, but what a terrible waste of valuable time it all was, bearing in mind that when a student is of an age and achievement to commence his first post, he will be entering a world which is utterly foreign to him.

At a factory such a person will be lost in trying to understand how the staff have to use their hands with skill. So much better off would he have been, had he been given the opportunity to use his own in similar work during the holidays. He will be lost, too, in the field of craft training. The junior apprentices will be unlikely to respect a young technician, no matter how brilliant, who is considerably less of a craftsman than they.

What will a highly skilled foreman think of the callow young man who seems hardly to know what he is talking about, yet has the status, or should have, of a " boss " figure? It is such aspects of working life, where an integral part of ability is ease in the conducting of relationships, that the Colleges of Advanced Technology foster. They are concerned with a fuller kind of maturity than that specifically of the brain.

Catching their students so young, the C.A.T.'s ensure that when, at the age of twenty-two or twenty-three, they finally leave, the students are considerably more than overgrown youths, have both feet planted firmly on the ground, have achieved their necessary qualifications and, above all, have been enabled to come to terms with the human element of working in a way no graduate from one of the generally accepted universities is likely to do.

Now, at last, the boy or girl temperamentally unsuited to formal academic training will not be denied a university degree, for in the Autumn of 1965 the first Technical University opened in Great Britain. It is the purpose-built Brunel University sited near Uxbridge, and it will be able to award a B.Tech. (Bachelor of Technology).

The students at Brunel will be self-selecting, people who have satisfied the examiners in the requisite number of "A" levels but know that they do not want to spend the next three years in purely formal study. They have a desire on the one hand to see the result of their calculations and, on the other, to work at these results as a team not of scientists like themselves, but with people from widely differing backgrounds from whom they can learn things not contained between the covers of a book or in a test tube.

Brunel is fortunate in being placed in the Western suburbs of London for this contains the biggest industrial area south of Birmingham with many differing types of industry. Students can, therefore, get local experience for at least one of their practical work placements, and throughout their training they will spend six months in college and six months in a factory. More time away from the university would, in the opinion of the Principal, cause them to lose contact and, to this end, contact by tutorials will be maintained during the period of separation. Tutors, in fact, will have to be conversant with all up-to-date technological processes so as to be up to the students when they return from the factories.

These " sandwich " courses were in operation when Brunel was functioning at Acton as a College of Advanced Technology, and received a certain amount of criticism. Tutors complained that as students settled down to hard study and learned the way to marshal their facts in a scholarly manner, or started on a small piece of research, they were uprooted again and became " workers " with not enough time to read. From the factory point of view it was found that such interruptions were bad for relations on the shop floor, and that just as the students were beginning to be accepted and trusted by their fellows and, thus, really be of use, they had to leave and become " college boys " again instead of men! Some of this criticism may be valid.

The Army has discovered that the officer who does best is one who spends a certain amount of time in the ranks, learning what the life of the ordinary soldier is like, and Brunel University will endeavour to apply this principle to industry. The medieval knight had to learn to ride, to use arms, to endure hardships, to serve his master, to mix also with the distinguished visitors to his master's table, showing them reverence and laughing at their feeble jokes. This was " education in the round " and perhaps it is time we learned this all over again.

This " complete " education would seem to have some interesting advantages, not the least of which is a marked lessening of emotional disorder. There are such disorders among students, but the over-all picture suggests that far less occurs when study is related to life in this way than is seen in the " traditional " universities. Perhaps this is due to the close contact between pupil and tutor, and the fact that problems can be discussed before they overwhelm.

Now that a Government Charter makes it possible for Colleges of Advanced Technology to assume the status of university, these " Universities with a Difference " will multiply. They are the melting pot for the sort of mentality that, until recently, was over-looked in the recognized fields of advanced education. They are certainly a short cut to the higher echelons of worldly success.

13

The Whole Child—A Postscript

THE field of education is a hot-bed of controversy. Sometimes it is not too difficult to believe that the multifarious statements appertaining to the education of gifted children, all boil down to single-mindedness amounting to egocentricity, in which the child is forgotten and the educationalist all-important.

This, of course, is a negative way of looking at the efforts of so many high-minded people, but on a more positive level we must be thankful that the children under review are being considered at all; are considered, indeed, important enough to provoke so much controversy.

However, there is an element of encapsulation in the attitude of some educationalists, a narrowness which, for instance, may result in an over-concern with the intellect at the expense of the emotions, or, inversely, an indulgence towards the sort of " free expression " which gives full rein to the element of anarchy which must exist in every child.

To take every aspect of a gifted child into account, mind, feelings, and body, would seem an ideal pre-occupation, but precious few people do seem to possess this encompassing attitude towards education which is, of course, education in the widest sense. An exception is Dartington Hall.

The philosophy which lies behind the curriculum of Dartington derives in part from the experiences of the chairman of trustees, Leonard Elmhurst. When serving in India during the First World War, he noticed that, despite the appalling poverty of villages, there seemed to survive an indestructible sense of community. When people are truly inter-dependent and can rely on one another, great strength can be drawn from the variety of relationships. Even in impoverished conditions, an astonishing level of contentment can be achieved.

In 1925, with the help of his wife, he purchased Dartington Hall in Devon. The Hall itself is in what remains a fine example in England of a 14th Century dwelling house. Part of the idea was a desire to show that with science and machinery the land could be made to pay, and that the drift from the village could be halted by the establishment of rural industries. Another part of these ideas was that a school should be established where children and adults might learn not only English and Latin, music and pottery, but how to live together in reasonable harmony.

The estate and the school are, today, an accomplished fact. The land is being farmed by modern methods, there are shops in which the tweeds made by the textile mill are sold, the woodland has been greatly enlarged, and a saw mill and a furniture factory provides work for many of the local population. Together, the group of enterprises show a profit on the investment.

Dartington Hall School was started in 1926, and then, as now, the aim was to provide an environment in which children can grow physically, intellectually and, most important of all, emotionally. That is why, with the rare exception due to circumstances, the youngest pupil is ten years old. He has, thus, been given the chance to establish the necessary and healthy parent-child relationship, the only true basis for an undisturbed development.

The real value of Dartington (which, incidentally, is co-educational) is that it offers a means of escape from the rigidity of a more stringently formal programme. With its great range of activities, it is an essential background to the unusually gifted child. To be brilliant in many directions has its drawbacks; a hungry man brought to a feast will hardly know what dish to tackle first. To be able to do many things brilliantly implies the need for an element of choice. But how does one choose without conflict, how does one avoid the fear that the wrong decision has been made, that one's real vocation was for something else?

Being a co-educational school provides certain problems, but these are modified, to a large extent, by the fact that a married couple are Co-Heads of the school. The exchange of ideas between the two heads and the respect that each accords the other seeps through to each and every pupil. The element of " war of the sexes " is diminished, in this way, to a remarkable degree. Probably no mixed collection of boys and girls in the country, at school, at home or where you will, seem to show such a concern for each other's point of view!

The difference between high intelligence and brilliance is the difference between the ability to expand in a conventional scholastic set-up, and the need for a far more specialized and yet elastic curriculum.

In this book, we are concerned with brilliance—achievement potentially at the top of the scale—and the limited amount of organizations available which are suited to enable brilliance to develop fully.

There are " pockets " of enlightened education, a few teachers scattered far and wide, well-equipped to handle brilliance, and in these chapters dealing with schools, some of them have been highlighted. But theirs are voices which should be heard in concert, and not, as is so often the case, individual voices shouting to the moon, up against prejudice and inhibiting orthodoxy.

The time must come, and the sooner the better, when the highly gifted child, right at the top of the intellectual ladder, is the centre of at least as much organized concern as his unfortunate educationally sub-normal brother, at the bottom.

14

The Under-achievers

C AN there be a greater gift than to be gifted? To contain
within oneself a miraculous chemistry, a physical and
emotional complex, which sharpens every aptitude we possess,
every facility we acquire? Then it is a terrible paradox that, by
virtue of this very innate blessing, the level of sensitivity is such
that sometimes we are the creators of our own, apparent, inadequacy, the instigators of our own downfall.

Negative forces of environment or heredity can play havoc with the
emotional structure of the gifted child, and can result in conditions
such as maladjustment, inconsequentialism, and possibly dyslexia.
But here, at this stage, our concern is with a lesser impairment—
the wasteful condition or under-achievement resulting in brilliant
youngsters who, at war with themselves, because of the failure of
others, made apathetic because their intelligence has not been
suitably exploited, have turned in the opposite direction and are
unable to learn. It is a form of delinquency which harms no-one
but themselves—that of the intellect.

Like the alcoholic, always promising to do better and consistently
failing to live up to the promise, the under-achiever is weakened
by deeper forces. He provokes the same mixture of tenderness
and exasperation as, indeed, the alcoholic. One feels, and there is
a nub of truth in it, that such children have an addiction of their
own—to not working. Every school report will show that they have
the capacity to understand (the occasional flash of brilliance is all
too apparent) but end of term results are, as usual, a sad
disappointment.

Regular work, like regular sleep, is a habit that has to be
acquired, but in the case of the gifted child, the habit of working

is harder to acquire for the following reason—his early responses at school or home are dulled by having too little to cope with.

In England, he will be five years old when he first attends school. Already, in many cases, he will have taught himself to read and, for the first time, he is out of the nursery class and in a " real " school. And where is the necessary stimulus that will live up to the excitement of such a drastic change in circumstances? It certainly does not come if the teacher expects him to start learning, all over again, a series of tasks that he may well have mastered at the age of three. Thus, boredom sets in.

Sometimes one forgets that all through his schooldays a child can be bored, and yet they can be and, indeed, often are. Boredom produces lack of interest, an excuse to daydream perhaps, anything other than listen to the drone of a voice explaining something which, to our clever child, needs no explanation at all.

And, suddenly, the teacher's eye is upon him. He is startled . . . confused . . . the question asked him does not register and he feels resentful and angry at being caught out, tripped up on a point which he could answer easily had he not been the victim of a sudden demand on his wandering attention.

The result? " For the benefit of John, we will have reading again " the teacher will say, or words to that effect, the unfortunate use of sarcasm deepening the already growing resentment. Worse, the " group "—the children around him—will, in their turn, feel resentment at his stupidity, his seeming inadequacy, making *them* the victims now, the ones who have got to do everything twice.

The child is father to the man. In later years, he will respond in the same way when in a similar situation and where he once let the class down (unnecessarily) he will now let the team down. The bright young recruit in the Army, trying to control his impatience with the almost monosyllabic explanation of how to load and cock a rifle, will stand there, confusing himself with his own ill-contained frustration, until suddenly it is his turn to demonstrate what has just been so painstakingly explained.

Needless to say, he is not ready. The flow of invective that this, seemingly, inadequate response invites only makes matters worse. Humiliation is the final ingredient in a complex of feelings which result in a show of impotence. " We'd all like to push off for our cup of tea and our currant bun, wouldn't we! " bellows the Sergeant " but we won't, my lad, we will stay here until the whole squad can perform this little task—AND THAT INCLUDES YOU! " This is not, of course, the best way to become popular amongst ones contemporaries!

" Angry silence " in the classroom, or " dumb insolence " on the parade ground, call them what you will, they are the same misconceptions on the part of the instructor. And they evince the same reaction on the part of the learner, a sense of injustice, and a determination to see the powers-that-be in hell first, rather than show the demanded response.

The result? Minimal achievement—just enough to keep the young student (or young soldier) out of trouble. And everybody is disappointed that one so obviously bright has done so very badly.

It is a vicious circle, very difficult to break. The solution, in the case of the child, is for his educators to know in advance the exceptional qualities of his mind. Parents can be forgiven for underestimating the intellectual needs of their children (especially when the parents are, as is sometimes the case, considerably less intelligent than their offspring) but teachers should, at least, be primed and ready for the possibility of encountering one or more highly gifted children in their classes.

There are ways in which even the most elementary of tasks can be opened up to suit the intellectual capacity of the child. The straightforward reading of a simple book can be something more than a bore to a clever child. He can be shown the way of using selection as a short cut to the acquirement of knowledge, instructed in the searching out of detail, asked to pick out words that " colour " rather than merely explain, and maybe even given a different, slightly more difficult, book to cope with.

This is not merely pandering to an exceptional demand. It is paving the way to a facility which can be of inestimable value at a later, more crucial, time. So many university students lack the facility to " skip " through a book, seizing on the salient points necessary for their studies. They have to plough through every single page, an unnecessary waste of time, and possibly a strain on their ability to sustain the necessary degree of interest. They could have learned how to "dispose" of non-applicable chapters, even paragraphs, by the early cultivation of an aptitude for selective reading from their earliest days at the first school they ever attended.

The full maturity of a mind from which high intelligence springs, is a condition which can bring the deepest satisfaction to the owner, and a uniquely valuable contribution to the world. That such a commodity as brilliance (for brilliance that can be applied successfully *is* a commodity of the highest value) should fail to be recognized, is a crime in itself. Unfortunately, it can amount to a crime against the potentially " rich " possessor of such brilliance:

CASE HISTORY

Robert was twelve years old, a slim dark-haired little boy, rather tall for his age. His father was a successful (from Robert's point of view *too* successful) businessman who had resented the fact that, along with many thousands of others, the war had taken five years out of his life.

His marriage had taken place in the immediate post-war period, and Robert's mother remembers that her husband had said: " I need *you* now, if I am to have time for all the things I want to do. We'll have children later, and by that time, my sons will have something to be proud of."

After the marriage, the young couple worked together, virtually, as a team. As the father had predicted, success began to come, the kind of success he had dreamed about while serving in the desert. They were making pre-fabricated buildings and houses, better in every way than the drab variety that had been rushed up during the " blitz." Homes, too, that could be assembled in a matter of hours. There were articles in the trade papers, pictures in the National dailies, enquiries from local authorities all over the country, even from other European countries that had been ravaged by war.

In the meantime, Robert had been born and, a couple of years later, a girl. The girl was the luckier of the two—she was extremely pretty, and over the years learned how to get what she wanted out of her father, even a high proportion of attention during the increasingly short time he spent at home. Robert despised the obvious methods she used, but although he needed as much overt affection, he also wanted to discuss " manly " things with his father, building methods for instance, the use of the new plastic materials, why one stood up to stress better than another. How it was that quick drying paint could not be used for certain export orders as it seemed to be affected more easily by changes of temperature, how these, and other difficulties, could be overcome.

Gifted children are always intensely interested in the things that go on around them, and Robert's intelligence was such that he wanted to talk, for instance, about how it felt to supply homes to people who would only live there for a short while before being moved to more permanent dwellings. After all, didn't his father say that families need roots, and that was why *his* family were going to stay where they were? Add to the home, maybe, but not move from it.

Robert had tried many times to get his father to talk about such things. At first it rather amused the man to see his son poring over trade journals that he had brought home and left lying around. He used to boast about this to his friends, but never in the boy's hearing. " It would be bad for him, make him much too cocky. Besides, how can a kid really understand? " (A striking case of under-estimation, or was it so that, at this period, the father unconsciously resented the child's interest? High intelligence in a child can be felt as a " threat " to the parent who is not completely secure in his self-belief.)

In the evening, when the father reached home, he was tired. It was more amusing to listen to the prattle of his small daughter. She only wanted to sit on his knee and have him read to her about the adventures of Noddy. So Robert virtually gave up trying to make contact with his father, and because we cannot " give up " on one front only, his school reports began to reflect his growing apathy in the acquirement of knowledge. Up to now they had been extremely good, but only the masters knew quite how good. Neither of the boy's parents realized that for him to be first or second in his form, term after term, bearing in mind the amount of " spare-time " reading he was doing, constituted an unusual achievement.

In the face of these ever more unsatisfactory school reports, Robert began to be nagged at by his father—apathy began to be deepened by resentment. But then there was a stroke of luck.

One of the father's business acquaintances (whose son attended the same school as Robert) came to lunch one Sunday. Robert's father grumbled to his visitor at the bad show his son was making at school nowadays, and how he wished to be proud of him. And then the whole family assembled for lunch.

During this, the two men began to talk " shop " and, primarily, the discussion centred around the difficulties attached to the electrical wiring of " prefabs " on the level of keeping down construction time—and Robert chipped in.

Under normal circumstances he would have been " shut up " by his father, but this could hardly occur in front of a guest. Instead of being told not to discuss matters which he could not possibly understand, he was given his head, so much so, that when the time came for the guest to depart, he made it quite clear that if *his* son, at the age of sixteen, knew as much about electrical matters as Robert, at the age of twelve, *he* would be proud!

" If he's working badly at school, there must be something wrong " said the guest. " Why don't you have a chat with the headmaster? " And Robert's father was too ashamed to admit that his only contact with his son's headmaster was a few words, once a year, on Sports Day. But he was genuinely concerned about the boy, and followed up this advice.

He was bewildered by what he heard. " An outstanding boy " said the Head. " Quite exceptional . . . interested in everything. Such good company, and so proud of you. Always talking to his friends about your work. His own seems to be suffering lately, and maybe he's a bit bored. I must see what I can do to get him more stimulating material."

Here was food for thought indeed. Robert's father began thinking seriously about his son, for the first time in the boy's life. Maybe he should take more interest in the boy. Maybe he should be allowed to feel slightly involved in his father's work.

But no dramatic decision was taken. The father did manage to spend more time with the boy and, much to his surprise, found he could talk to him almost like an equal. He started to feel that his son was a friend. Whenever it was possible, he took the boy with him on business trips.

Robert was, indeed, lucky. The home climate changed, just in time, and he was prevented from sinking completely into the committed apathy of the under-achiever.

The above case history illustrates, only too clearly, that notwithstanding the most enlightened educational facilities, a stable and developing personality can only occur when the home situation is satisfactory. There is no doubt that under-achievement, precipitated originally by too low a level of educational challenge, is only, indeed, *precipitated,* but not originated. Something is wrong in a far deeper level.

The story of Robert is a classically clear example of the failure to be recognized for ones true worth by the father. Sometimes, unfortunately, lack of recognition can arise from the physical absence of the parent due either to work or to marital problems. A man who spends his leisure hours with the lads in the local pub, rather than face the evenings with his family, is insufficiently in evidence to meet the needs of a very young son.

A child needs to identify with the parent of his or her own sex, before any internal effort can be made to live up to his potential. In the case of a marriage gone wrong, and the father's absence, it is not impossible that a sympathetic substitute may perform this necessary paternal function; a " friend " of the mother, even an uncle who is around sufficiently to take an active interest in the lad and, in return, receive some of the affection that a child needs to give.

The male child of a widowed mother is up against this problem, although if the child was old enough, before the father died, to have successfully passed through this process of identification, the very absence of the father could provide the necessary spur to achieve maturity. (" Daddy is dead. I must take his place.") But, of course, this can then create the different problem of overattachment to the mother, and produce, at a later age, a different form of emotional immaturity.

A girl is not up against the same problem, for the obvious reason that she usually remains with her mother, and also it is socially permissible for a woman to entertain friends of her own sex. The important difference is, of course, that educationally at least, the majority of girls are not required to achieve the same degree of excellence as their male counterparts.

There is no substitute for a stable home background, and it cannot be too strongly emphasized that here lie the seeds of the gifted child's failure to live up to his potential. Even when a widowed mother attempts to reconstruct the *materially* conducive background to a child's educational progress, all sorts of problems can occur. Imagine the recently widowed mother of a gifted child, determining to continue the child's education. Perhaps she will go to work to bring in the necessary money. Her absence may mean the child will have to go to a boarding school. Thus, the mother's working pattern establishes itself, and she finds herself up against the strain of keeping a good job *and* looking after a home. When the child is at home, during school holidays, far from being able to give him that much more attention, her wearing activities make her less tolerant of childish shortcomings. Not only is the father absent, but the mother is being less than a mother for all her attempts to be both father *and* mother.

In such circumstances, the enlightened teacher can perform an invaluable function, above all, in giving the child a degree of sympathetic attention above that necessary for one less deprived. The possibility of a warm and reciprocal relationship between teacher and pupil, in such a situation, could be the saving factor in the healthy intellectual development of the young pupil.

It must be remembered that in the case of a fatherless child, the predisposition towards under-achievement is strong. The habit of working needs extra encouragement. Not to have one's intellectual needs met at school, plus the emotional satisfaction absent from the home, is loading the dice against the possibility of educational achievement.

Finally, it must always be taken into account that the failure to meet a child's needs, no matter on what level, produces a sense of injustice which can only deepen over the years. Not to be recognized for one's worth can lead to aggression directed against one's parents, teachers and, ultimately, against the very concept of authority.

From whom, then, can the growing child learn?

15

The Dyslexics

" I HAVE been perturbed for some time by a small number of children, and boys in particular, who are having abnormal difficulties in spelling. They consistently scramble their letters and do not relate letter to sound . . ." This note to Dr. Bannatyne at The Dyslexic Children's Centre of The Invalid Children's Aid Association was written by the headmaster of a large comprehensive school.

The headmaster had taken the trouble to write to experts and not dismissed these problem children as lazy, or indifferent or sub-normal, or just about anything else other than what they were —victims of specific dyslexia.

It is only comparatively recently that the condition of, as it is commonly called, word-blindness has been recognized for what it is: a conceptual deficiency for which there is no quick cure although these children can be taught to read given great patience and understanding on the part of therapist and teacher.

Even in the face of what would appear to be foolproof, many doctors and educators refuse to believe there is such a condition as Specific Dyslexia. All manner of reasons are given to account for the inability, to a greater or lesser degree, to read and write, the most commonly put forward being a failure of maturation which, of course, implies that when the obstacles accounting for such a failure are removed, or outgrown, the deficiency will lessen in the natural course of events.

Unfortunately this is not the case, and rather than the number of sufferers of word blindness decreasing as generalized inhibitions are lifted, it is now feared that many boys and girls who are assumed to be the victims of no more than a failure of maturation will, indeed, have to be included among the continuing sufferers, no matter how clever, even brilliant, they may be in all other respects. For to suffer from this condition implies no lack of intelligence. It can, and does, exist where the level of intelligence puts the dyslexic child into the genius class.

Reading is so much part of our lives that it is difficult for us to imagine what it is like not to be able to read or write with any degree of facility. For so long these two skills have been equated with intelligence (or lack of it) that when a child has difficulty in learning them at school, he is only too readily thought of as " backward."

Specific Dyslexia first became known to the medical profession through patients who had suffered some degree of brain injury and were unable to understand the written word for some time afterwards. A well known consultant engineer described to one of the authors how, during an experiment he was conducting when a young man, he sustained a six hundred volt shock. Luckily there were other people nearby who came to his aid and in an hour or two he seemed perfectly well except for some stiffness of the arms and legs, but he was for a short time unable to make sense of the written word. In such a case the patient, through a temporary brain trauma, reverts for a while to the condition which, in the case of a dyslexic, is permanent.

The word " dyslexia " was first used by Professor Berlin of Stuttgart University in a monograph published in 1887 and since then much work has been done on this subject by neurologists, but until recently it had not been realized that if the word-blind child is to be helped at all, a team approach is needed in which the neurologist, psychologist and specially trained teacher are working together to help him.

Like spastics, word-blind children have often been classed as defective when they reached school and their parents, unless exceptionally persistent in their search for treatment and their conviction that the child was of normal intelligence, have been forced to agree with the harassed teacher: (" He is so far behind the others in reading and writing that he doesn't seem to have grasped anything about them since he came to school.") But herein lies the crux of the problem—teachers have never been instructed to recognize the difference between the spelling of the child who is sub-normal and that of the dyslexic, whose spelling is in a scrambled class of its own.

Dr. Macdonald Critchley, one of the foremost authorities on this subject, gives examples of this spelling in his book on Developmental Dyslexia published in 1964:

"*Forg all fore oy miney.*" (for "Fred had five white mice" written to dictation by a boy of 9 years).

"*Lash Monday we went to the zoo. We spent much time in frunt of an ion cag with hal senner mahgen they made us lrfe wen they put out they pouis for nuts.*"

(for "Last Monday we went to the zoo. We spent much time in front of an iron cage which held seven monkeys. They made us laugh when they put out their paws for nuts," written to dictation by a boy of eleven years).

"*Can w kip a man way goob.*" ("Can you keep a man who wants to go" written to dictation by a girl aged twenty-one.)

From these examples, it will be seen that the spelling mistakes made by dyslexic children are quite different from those made by defectives, or ordinary children who have been ill-educated. Dyslexics telescope words and certain letters are much more likely to be omitted than others. Hermann of the Ordblinde Institut at Copenhagen, who has made a study of this condition among Danish children, noted that vowels and mute letters were most likely to be dropped, and English psychologists have noted that the dyslexic child tends to spell phonetically. This means that with the curiosities of the English language (trough and through, plough and brow) children in England are even more at a disadvantage, when suffering from this disability, than they might be in, for instance, Finland or Germany, although the German child also gets into terrible muddles with his portmanteau words when these are telescoped.

Usually the writing of dyslexics is very untidy; capital letters appear at random, and letters are persistently reversed. NOT may be spelt TNO or ONT or TON and there is no consistency in the way that these are used. It is this apparent inability to learn from past mistakes that leads teachers to think that such a child is dull and cannot learn. It so happens that the dyslexic child will often " forget " what a word or letter looks like even in the middle of a sentence, when he has just used the very word on the line above. It is no wonder that an uninstructed teacher, faced with one or two such submissions in several hundred exam papers, may feel that a pupil's grasp of The Wars of the Roses cannot be very great if it is presented as " t wrs f t rsss," and written in a way that makes the bizarre spelling almost unreadable.

For the highly intelligent child, dyslexia is a serious handicap, both emotionally and from the point of view of learning. Most children with I.Q.'s of 140 and over learn to read early, usually between the ages of four and five, and many even younger, and the very fact of acquiring this skill is of immense value to them, inasmuch as they can find out for themselves the answers to, at least, some of the questions which they are always asking, and which their parents may be too busy or uninformed to answer. But the gifted non-readers are frustrated to an intense degree and when they, ultimately, go to school, the other children seem much brighter by comparison.

It is not much use being able only to answer the verbal questions in class. The spoken word is ephemeral and those that use them, such as actors, easily forgotten as compared with those with a gift for the written word. Thus, the gifted dyslexic, with his inability to write, cannot make the permanent record his thinking deserves, and he may well become discouraged and feel himself a complete failure, taking refuge in daydreaming and fantasy. Owing to the normal need for acceptance by the " group " such a child may turn to clowning in order to get the attention his achievement should bring, and so cause disturbance in class. For this, naturally, he will be punished with the concomitant increase in anxiety that punishment brings in its wake and therefore it is even more difficult for him to make use of the little literary skill he does possess. The older he gets, the more difficult it becomes for him to make progress with his studies, which come progressively to depend more and more on the written word.

A dyslexic boy of seventeen years, known to the authors, illustrates this point. Both the parents are mathematicians, and both are engaged in University work. They live on the outskirts of the town, books line the walls, friends and students of the father drift in and out and there is a continual exchange of ideas. The boy's I.Q. is in the region of 170 but might be even higher as tests at this level cannot be properly standardized owing to the small number in this group, plus the fact that his dyslexia makes ordinary testing very difficult. He has one sister two years older than he is and, from the first, the children were noticed to be very different from each other. The girl was much more " sensible," seemed at ease both with children of her own age and with her parents' friends, was quick and neat in her movements, and enjoyed games. The boy was always slow, and found it much more difficult to make friends. The parents realized early that the child was well above average intelligence, but at that time word-blindness had not been properly recognized as such and schools where remedial teaching could be given were even fewer than now. The boy went first to a small day school, and then to a nearby prep school which proved disastrous, for he made hardly any progress with his reading, his writing was appallingly bad, his work smudged and untidy. Gradually he became more and more unhappy, although he had gleaned much knowledge through being read to by his mother.

Eventually he refused to go to school at all. He taught himself to read after a fashion, for he had a tremendous drive to study mathematics and scientific subjects, but he failed his 11 + and his further education was a serious problem. At last, the father heard of a public school where the head was interested in high I.Q. children with or without problems and was acquainted with the condition of dyslexia. The boy went there at the age of twelve and made good progress and ultimately managed to gain a scholarship to University. But even with the remedial teaching he is still receiving, he may be prevented from taking up the scholarship, as he still has difficulty in English and will have to pass this at " O " level.

If he fails to pass, he will be denied the education, owing to his handicap, that his age, ability and aptitude fit him for. Luckily his mathematical gifts are so outstanding that he will undoubtedly be able to make use of them, although he will be denied the opportunity of mixing with the stimulating company that a University course provides. Yet compared to many dyslexics, the boy is lucky inasmuch as he is being given the opportunity to develop to whatever degree he is capable of, notwithstanding his drawback.

Another example is quoted by Dr. Macdonald Critchley and concerns a girl of eighteen, a member of a dyslexic family and severely retarded in learning to read. By dint of great application, coupled with a background of high intelligence, she largely mastered her disability, although she never learned to spell correctly. A brilliant musical executant, she was considerably handicapped at the Royal College of Music because of her persistent inability to read musical notation.

She, like the boy, chose a subject in which they could excel and where actual reading is reduced to a minimum, for symbols of other kinds are used. Other children, similarly affected, are less fortunate.

Many famous people were, we now realize, dyslexics, Hans Christian Andersen for instance. He could not cope with his ordinary school work and was thought by his teachers to be dull. He never learned to spell and most of the mistakes in his manuscripts had to be corrected by proof readers. A clue to his disability occurred when he wrote of his visit to Charles Dickens in London for he spelt the names of many people and places incorrectly and as his proof reader did not know English perfectly, the mistakes were allowed to stand.

Karl XIth of Sweden was almost certainly dyslexic. Despite being known as one of Sweden's wisest kings, he never learned to read properly and always relied on the spoken word. If a report came in, he often held the paper upside down and pretended to read it. His spelling was of the kind found in dyslexic children, words were reversed, letters missed, and there were the usual bizzare abbreviations. It is tempting to continue the list, and one wonders whether Leonardo da Vinci was a dyslexic. He left little written work, wrote a kind of shorthand and used drawings to illustrate his thoughts whenever possible. Perhaps he was able to call upon his immense gifts to compensate for a deficiency in the more conventional mediums of communication.

In Denmark, special teaching for dyslexics has been available for the past thirty years. At Copenhagen, the Ordblinde Institut has been operating since 1936. When Danish children first enter school, the reading and writing rate is carefully watched, and if a child proves very slow, yet is known to be intelligent, he is sent to a special class within the school where there are only about fifteen to each teacher. If he still fails to respond and is diagnosed as being a developmental dyslexic, then he is sent to the Institut. Transport is provided, and lodgings arranged for those children who live too far away to make this practicable.

The children are between nine and ten years old by the time they are admitted, and they stay for about two years, after which most of them can cope well enough to re-enter the ordinary school system. Tuition goes on for about six hours a day in addition to reading and writing which are, of course, the main subjects, and is given to very small groups of three children to one teacher although arithmetic is taught in larger groups, while there are also handicrafts, music and drawing. All the teachers have undergone special post-graduate training and are interested in the problem. If the child needs further help, he can enter the continuation centre. The Institut can take a hundred children at a time while certain teachers are specially trained and are able to undertake private instruction.

Various teaching techniques are used, and as it has been universally found that the look-and-say method makes reading more difficult for these children, a phonetic system is practised. All kinds of visual aids are employed and everything is done to make the material interesting to the pupils.

In England, the problem has been recognized at last, and although much work is being done, this is still only scratching the surface. In 1958, the John Horniman School was set up. It is a boarding school in Sussex for children with severe speech and language difficulties. Many of these children also have emotional problems, and this aspect has to be dealt with before the young pupils can devote their energy to the over-riding consideration. Although there is a divergence of opinion as to the exact cause of difficulty of communication generally, and of developmental dyslexia in particular, most people believe that it is not purely emotional or psychological and that if these aspects are recognized, it certainly makes it much easier for the child to cope with his learning difficulties.

In 1964 the present Centre for dyslexic children was established in London. This has three main functions . . . (1) to diagnose developmental dyslexics, and for this purpose, medical, neurological and special psychological tests are given. (2) To provide special teaching for those children who have been diagnosed. The children attend at regular intervals but still spend most of their time in ordinary schools as, at present, it is felt of importance that they do not lose touch with their own age group or their difficulties might be exacerbated. (3) Research (based on the children actually seen) into the cause of dyslexia, including interviews with parents as the condition seems to be largely hereditary, and there is often a direct or indirect background of dyslexic symptoms.

The Centre will move into larger and better equipped premises (summer 1965) and then the numbers can be increased to about fifty which is the optimum number for the present staff. The project that is perhaps dearest to the heart of Dr. A. D. Bannatyne, Ph.D., the psychologist in charge, is the training of teachers in modern methods of coping with dyslexic pupils, so that help can be given in primary schools, at the time indeed when such a need is first recognized, so that emotional difficulties due to non-recognition of the condition can be obviated.

Dr. Bannatyne has a small number of gifted children and finds them most stimulating to teach. One bright boy, attending a well-known public school, has invented a record player in which the record does not have to be turned over. He shows the inventiveness of so many of the gifted, but he still has to face his " O " levels and

" A " levels if he is to gain further education. To do this, he needs the specialized help he is obtaining from the Centre.

What should the astute teacher look for to enable the earliest possible diagnosis of dyslexia to be made? Above all, of course, the seemingly incredible schism between the general intelligence and the inability to read and write. Having satisfied themselves that there is no emotional barrier to account for the condition, the teacher or therapist can then recognise various manifestations which vary, to a greater or lesser degree, not only in general intensity, but even from day to day.

There is a tendency to fail in the recognition between left and right. A child suffering from specific dyslexia occasionally attempts to read whole lines backwards. A variation of this in writing is the " mirror " form of writing, in which words are written as though reflected in a mirror. The latter symptom is, it so happens, not uncommon in the normal development of children, but when it persists into adolescence, something is obviously wrong.

A remarkable although very rare symptom is to do with what is known as a spatial failure, and this is bound up with the inability to distinguish between left and right. " Now John " says the therapist, " touch the middle finger of my left hand with the index finger of your right hand." Young John looks perplexed. He knows what is his right hand and he knows too what is the index finger. He studies the hands of the therapist. His problem is to be able to " place " her left hand in relation to his right hand. A sense of confusion grows in his mind. He twists his body as if to stand behind her, and make the comparison this way.

Ah, he's got it . . . he knows which is the left hand, so he reverts to his original position—and in the fraction of time necessary to do this, he has already forgotten, and he begins to twist and turn in an agonized attempt to recapture the now forgotten insight. To watch such a display is to realize the degree of despair which an intelligent child must experience in the (one would have thought) simple process of distinguishing between left and right.

Another very revealing symptom is the uncertainty of eye movements when following a short sentence written vertically, something as elementary as "today is a nice day, the rain has stopped." A machine exists for photographing these eye movements. Those of the dyslexic show a wild and random movement in contrast with the purposeful rhythm of the control groups. Thus we have an indication of the pathetic uncertainty of the dyslexic when attempting to read a simple sentence.

The day to day problems of the youngster who suffers from this crippling condition can be enormous. Imagine a young adolescent taking his first girl out to a meal in a café. There they sit, she wearing her new dress, he with his hair slicked back neatly, both studying the menu. At least, *she* is studying it, he is merely looking at a meaningless jumble of black and white lines, and hoping against hope that she will not ask him what he has chosen.

It is for such reasons that dyslexics, especially those of good intelligence should be recognized for what they are. Sympathy and understanding will help them, not only to overcome their disability, but to accept it so they can also concentrate on other gifts to make up for the lack. Often a blind man has unusually acute hearing, and someone who is deaf is able to learn to lip-read. There is no reason, given the basic intelligence or gifts, why a sufferer from specific dyslexia should not become a successful lawyer, or surgeon, and indeed such cases exist.

Once again, as in so many other conditions, the importance of early diagnosis cannot be over-emphasized. It could mean the difference between a life of reasonable fulfilment and a life of tragic frustration. As yet, few teachers have been trained to recognize the signs. Even the cause (or causes) of dyslexia is not certain. What *is* certain is that such children need specialized help, and their families instructed in supplementing such help if their innate intelligence is not to be wasted by the failure in harnessing it to recognized channels of communication.

16

The Inconsequentials

<hr style="width:10%"/>

THE term "inconsequential" is comparatively new in the science of the mind, but it describes graphically the general attitude of irresponsibility, which is the hallmark of its victims; for victims they are. Of significance is the fact that many of them had difficult births and probably are victims, too, of minimal brain damage—the very condition that decompression is believed to obviate.

The "inconsequential" is the child who lives for the immediate moment, taking little if anything into account which must be to its detriment. Danger is no deterrent—it cannot relate cause to effect. A future, even in terms of seconds, would not seem to exist. Indeed, any known pattern of existence, any purposefulness, is conspicuous by its absence. Such a child must act without considering the consequences.

A reasonably trained dog will hesitate before crossing a busy road—it has learned that a car can be a killer—but the inconsequential child would seem to be aware only of its desire to cross the road. Nothing else matters but the immediate gratification of the immediate need. It will not wait—perhaps *cannot* wait—it has never learned the lesson of caution, of self-preservation. Several years of journeying to school alone, and negotiating traffic-bound roads in the process, will teach it nothing.

In class restlessness is one of the most outstanding characteristics of the inconsequential. He fidgets with his pencil, drops it to the floor, then makes a great clatter and disturbance in order to retrieve it. Unable to concentrate, he will pull aimlessly at a shirt cuff until this tears, thus ensuring trouble immediately he gets through the

RIGHT: Height-finding apparatus
in the study of trees

BELOW: Gathering material for
a written survey

BELL OF THE
BEAUMONDE
WRECKED WITH
CARGO OF WINE 1881.

BEAU-MONDE
ST JOHN

Photo: *Sevenoaks Chronicle*

Gifted spastic children
conquer their tragic
disability

Photo: *J. L. Allwork Ltd.*

door of his home! In the meantime, of course, nothing has been learned, no work has been done, so it is not surprising that many inconsequential children are thought by their teachers and parents to be stupid or of low intelligence.

Even when the child's innate intelligence is recognized, there seems to be no way of reaching him, because his attention span is so limited. " I know he can understand but he won't listen! " cry his teachers, goaded into frustration by the spectacle of a potentially brilliant child wasting time and energy in a catalogue of meaningless pursuits, and disturbing the entire class in the process. For easy distractibility is one of the features of this condition together with the difficulty of fixing attention on anything for more than a few moments. Thus what is normal in very young children puts the inconsequential into the wasted group of " emotionally retarded."

This emotional immaturity is sometimes called psychopathy when it occurs in adults—adults so far as chronological age is concerned. They, like the inconsequential child, are fairly easy to recognize but almost impossible to treat, and have the same effect of rousing exasperation in all with whom they come into contact. They have retained their infantile ways of response.

So often they are superficially likeable to an extraordinary degree. They can " charm the lid off a saucepan " to get what they want, a characteristic which is, frequently, all they have to get them through life. They have never been able to learn anything else. Which of us has not lent money to a " friend " for what one hopes, and yet knows, is not for the last time, because once again the story of temporary setback seems so convincing? At school, the clever but inconsequential child may have similar stories to account for a failure in learning which seems to bear no relation to his high intelligence.

This kind of lying in which the subject, or certainly a part of him, believes to be as true as he would like others to believe, is part of his character, and is fantasy at a very childish level. When a four year old looks into the garden and tells one solemnly that " there are two tigers under the rose bush," one does not, if one is wise, insist that it is " our cat and the cat next door," but tries

6

to make sure that a large part of the child knows it is all a game which is fun to play. To be able to indulge in such colourful fantasy, and yet to be able to separate it from reality, is an acquirement which can give great pleasure throughout life. But the inconsequential child insists on the reality of this fantasy-lie, and will cry and scream with misery at the thought that he is not believed. He *has* to be believed . . . black *has* to be white.

In the case of a nine year old, such a reaction stems from the deepest insecurity. Correction to his fantasy is seen as a threat to his very existence, and not as a help towards self-knowledge. Temper tantrums are very common in such children and they are capable of damaging either themselves or any property around them. The tendency to destruction in adolescence may well originate in an " inconsequential " childhood.

Aggression is part of all of us, and only controlled by social maturity which dictates to us the ways in which it can be permissibly expressed. For instance, the deliberate smashing of crockery can bring tremendous relief, whether at a stall at a country fair where we allow ourselves to do it with wooden balls sold to us by the Vicar, or, as with Osbert Sitwell, with a pile of plates handed him one by one by his housekeeper and smashed by him on a tiled floor to express his frustration when the cab he ordered did not turn up to take him to breakfast with a painter friend in Fitzroy Street. Both of these are " permitted " ways of dealing with frustration, but the inconsequential will not see the difference between these and slashing the seats of the railway carriage. His total disregard for the feelings and property of others, and his inability to connect such actions with their retributive consequences, seems to be at variance with his high intelligence. When he comes into contact with the law, he is the despair of the Probation Officer. He only knows, but does not feel, that he has done wrong. There is no emotional " brake " to his behaviour.

We all have a threshold of frustration but that of the inconsequential child is practically on the floor. He cannot bear to be thwarted, and as we are all thwarted many times a day the inconsequential continually finds himself at odds with his fellows. His high intelligence shows him the way to overcome the enemy in a game of cops and robbers, but by the time his slower witted friends have grasped the idea (which he is too impatient to explain to them in order that his plan may be understood) the moment has passed, and he curses them; no one is less able to suffer fools gladly—he cannot suffer them at all, and thus he becomes isolated from his fellows and develops the " Miller of Dee " syndrome . . . " I care for nobody, no, not I, and nobody cares for me." And, of course, the only sufferer is himself.

Yet he desperately craves affection and admiration from the very "peer" group from which he has just been at great pains to detach himself by his behaviour, his inability to tolerate. He mustn't feel humility, he mustn't care, an attitude which is kept up at all costs and no punishment in the ordinary sense can touch him. A mother will say " his father has thrashed the living daylights out of him, but it doesn't make any difference, there is nothing else we can do." Or the Magistrate will deliver a pious lecture on the importance of respecting other people's property and the offence will be repeated immediately the boy leaves the Detention Centre to which he has been sent to teach him a lesson. He cannot be taught a lesson, because he is unable to learn.

The normal child gradually learns from experience; this is part of growing up, this social ability to learn from our mistakes. But not so the inconsequential child, who continues to make the same mistakes. So he will trade on his charm to get him out of the difficulties into which, on his own reckoning, he has fallen quite by chance and, when on the rare occasion this does not work, he will be filled with angry disbelief that such an unfair punishment should be visited on him by " them." Then he will go to the other extreme and do his best to destroy the image of himself he has just built, but to no avail. Refusing to be helped to extricate himself from a situation which no-one but he has created, he throws himself back again into the pit, dragging with him all who have tried to help, so those who care most about him are the ones who suffer most.

Perhaps it is in his family relationships that the inconsequential child first meets disaster. A baby, first, learns the difference between himself and the breast, between himself and his mother, and then strives to please that he may be rewarded with her smiles and caresses as part of his normal development, but not the inconsequential. They remain the prisoners of their own immediate desires, they cannot differentiate between themselves and others. No-one else must have an existence, because in a position of dependency, this implies possible sanctions, possible refusals and, consequently, unbearable frustration. This results in a self-concern of such impregnability that no-one else can possibly matter, so no genuine give-and-take relationship can be formed. Everything, even love, is conducted on the most superficial and childish level. Just as the child of between five and ten attending his junior school will have a best friend that changes every week or two, apparently for trivial reasons, so the inconsequential child at a much older age will be unable to keep his friends, although when questioned will always reel off a list of names; he is longing for acceptance by the " group " but unable to do anything, to *give* anything, to get it. He cannot be loyal either to himself or to others and will betray any confidence to make a good tale or draw the attention of a newly met acquaintance. This is part of their " Here and Now " mentality; all desire must be satisfied at once, however impossible this may be, at whatever the cost to the future.

Parents, especially mothers, are always making excuses for affectionally impaired children, but always know that they are different from the others. " Never was one to show any affection. John used to like me to tuck him up at night, but Bobby never did, used to turn away from me, he did, although he was always jealous of John, used to make him swap toys with him although his Dad and I were ever so careful and always bought them things as near alike as we could, and spent the same amount of money on them." So right from the beginning, the inconsequential high I.Q. child becomes something of an isolate.

The distribution of such children is, of course, one that cuts across all social classifications and can occur at any income level. It is just as bewildering for the housemaster at a prep school to have a boy of ten who cannot bear to be passed over for a place in the team although manifestly not good enough, (or for the same boy to burst into angry tears when he is beaten in a game of table tennis) as for the junior school class teacher to have a boy who is convinced that he should play the lead in the Christmas play although he hasn't bothered to learn his part or turn up for rehearsals.

Research is going on in Great Britain and in other countries into the recognition of these children, and not a day too soon, because the wastage in potential applied intelligence, due to such immaturity is tragic. The man who has done most in this field is Dr. D. H. Stott, of Glasgow University, who postulates that the mothers of inconsequential children may have had troubled pregnancies and that the children may, in fact, be very slightly brain damaged. He suggests that inconsequential behaviour is a failure of temporal integration at the stage where the situation is appraised. In other words, the total inability of the child to judge a certain situation and act accordingly once this judgement has been made. Truly an interference at the very seat of judgement. He thinks that this inability is due to some impairment of the neural structures within the brain so that only the immediate situation and the immediate goal is taken into account. In these circumstances, therefore, we can begin to see why sometimes a child's actions seem to be totally against his own interests as, for instance, refusal to clean the family car or take on a paper round which could earn him the money to go with the class to Paris—a trip that he was longing to make.

Dr. Stott agrees that high intelligence does not appear to modify this behaviour in any way, and that owing to the need to seek attention from others in their own age group, the inconsequential child will pay any price. Lack of judgement can lead him easily into delinquent behaviour directed against the very teacher with whom, paradoxically, he may also have the wish and the need to stand well. This same minimal brain damage is held to account for the inability to learn from experience, the hypothesis being that where such a condition exists, there is no cerebral record, as with normal people, to be produced at will from the filing cabinet of " recall." Thus a situation repeated always amounts to a fresh experience; nothing has been recorded to help modify its effect.

There are however many differing opinions about the cause of inconsequential behaviour in children, and just as many about the cause of psychopathic behaviour in adults. Dr. Stott wishes to emphasize that though the inconsequential child has many traits in common with the psychopath, they are not to be totally equated, but they are both, like the elephant, easy to recognize when one meets them a second time, although very hard to describe convincingly to others.

Dr. David Stafford-Clark, Physician in Charge of the Department of Psychological Medicine at Guy's Hospital, says " The psychopathic personality represents a failure of maturation of personality whose impact is evident not so much in the mind or feeling of the patient as in his conduct, and particularly in his failure to make an effective adjustment with the rest of society. This is the fundamental abnormality of the psychopath, and although characteristically independent of any degree of intellectual impairment or mental defect, it corresponds in terms of personality development to a failure to emerge beyond the explosive period of early infantile development." He stresses that this failure to mature can be seen in a number of different ways. The E.E.G. (electroencephalograph) tends, when measuring electric impulses from the brain, to be dominated by waves and distribution normally seen only in children below the age of five. Capillary structure directly visible through the skin of the nail bed shows a corresponding preponderance of infantile forms. According to Dr. Stafford-Clark, the causes of this condition are multiple, " hereditary, constitutional and environmental. The hereditary component is difficult to assess but is probably due to multifactorial recessive genes; the constitutional element is undoubted and will often account for the emergence of a psychopathic personality in one member of the family where paternal relationships and siblings are apparently normal in every respect. The striking lack of correlation with intellectual development remains unexplained." The actual diagnosis of psychopathic personality is used by psychiatrists for adults rather than for children, as many of the character traits are part of the natural process of growing up. For instance no mother is surprised at having to call her seven year old more than once on a cold morning and urge him to be in time for school, but if at seventeen this is still necessary and results in the loss of one job after another, something is badly wrong. It is only when no more progress towards emotional maturity seems possible that the term should be used.

Two eminent authorities, therefore, believe that there is a physical factor, however slight, to account for the behaviour of the inconsequential child and the adult psychopath; both agree that such people have failed to mature emotionally and socially and emphasize that the condition is not a mental illness in the conventional sense of the word, but would seem to spring from some essential lack in personality integration.

Another explanation of this kind of behaviour in the gifted child is given by Dr. John Bowlby, a Consultant child psychiatrist and Director of the Tavistock Clinic, who says that children who are deprived of continuous maternal care and love during the first few years of life often develop into the Affectionless Child, in whom the growth towards maturity seems to have been halted. He also thinks that this deprivation may account for some juvenile delinquency; during the research for his book *Forty-four Juvenile Thieves* he found the common factor was that all the children had been separated from their mothers for more than a week or two before the age of five years and that they may have become damaged as a result. Ironically enough, it does not seem to matter whether the separation is by accident or design; whether deliberate desertion, or the fact that the mother has had to leave home to care for a dying relative. Dr. Bowlby found that faulty or delayed maturation often occurs when a very small child is admitted to hospital, even for what is clinically a minor operation. A child under the age of four, whether gifted or not, has no sense of time. It is no use saying " Mummy will come to visit on Tuesday," or even tomorrow, for time means nothing, although absence means everything. It means desertion, it implies that love does not exist and therefore distrust of parents frequently occurs, and there is no reassurance when the next visit does materialize, for what has happened once can happen again. " If I don't care, I can't be hurt," thinks, or rather " feels " the young patient, and an affectionless life begins.

Luckily for most children visiting times in children's wards have now been much extended, mainly due to the work done by Dr. Bowlby and Dr Ronald MacKeith, Consultant Paediatrician. Very often mothers may visit at any time, and in some cases are admitted with the children if their family circumstances permit. This is an attempt to cut down the period of fear and separation, and thus mitigate later behaviour difficulties. One must not forget that a gifted child is often born with an emotional skin missing and so is more susceptible to the " east wind of maternal deprivation."

Are there any ways in which we can compensate children for their feelings that they have been deprived of love? Sometimes when a second child is born the first will regress, that is his behaviour will become much more childish. If he has just learned to feed himself or not to wear a nappy at night, he will insist on being fed and start bedwetting, both habits a trial to the busy mother concerned with the new baby. She will, however, in most cases, quickly realize what is wrong and allow him the extra care he needs, and once again he is secure and can begin to grow up.

In the Children's Village of Skåo, near Stockholm, much older children are allowed to regress to infancy, even to the stage of taking their milk out of babies' bottles. They are then encouraged to form close relationships with the House Father and Mother, on whom they become extremely dependent for a time. This is deliberate policy, carrying calculated risks, but with these inconsequential children ordinary methods are useless as the therapist must use the relationship he has with the child in the treatment situation, and these children do not seem to have been able to form relationships.

The inconsequentials do in fact present an almost insoluble problem and together with exasperation and frustration, they arouse a feeling of helplessness in all who try to deal with them. The letter that follows was received by one of the authors from a colleague asking whether there was anything else she could have done for the subject, her student:

Mary H. arrived at her Northern Teacher Training College with a very good academic record; she clearly was a gifted girl, aged $18\frac{1}{2}$, and seemed likely to cope well with her Course. She was a little under average height, pleasant featured and with a slim boyish figure. (*note*: Physical immaturity is often seen in gifted children, especially those who are emotionally retarded.) Her hair was cut short and curled round her head. She told me that she had had an abscess at the back of her neck, and that her hair had been cut for ease of treatment on one side, but that " in order not to look lop-sided " she had decided on a short crop all over. On the evening of her fourth night in college, she came to me, very much upset, and asked " Should a male Tutor make jokes about my hair?"

I tried to play this down as I knew the man concerned to be kindly and sympathetic and certainly popular with most of the students. We talked for some time, and Mary gave as an explanation as to why she had applied for Teacher Training on a chance vacancy the fact that, when she left school at seventeen, she had not the slightest idea what she wanted to do, and had tried secretarial work, nursing, and also worked as a shop assistant before deciding that the one thing she wanted to do was to teach.

I thought this fairly reasonable as the qualities needed for one profession are by no means the same as for another, but I did feel that she had made rather heavy weather of a chance remark, regarding her hair, about which she had complained.

Mary shared a bed-sitting room with another student. Next morning, a message reached me from her room-mate . . . " Mary has tried to commit suicide!"

When I investigated, I found that the overdose of sleeping tablets had been such that cold water on her face and a couple of cups of black coffee were all it had taken to revive her, and, in any case, the fact of sharing a room made early discovery inevitable. She then admitted, very tearfully, that in the time between leaving school and coming to college she had received a good deal of psychiatric treatment, some of it as an in-patient, but that she had not seen fit to disclose this information.

The girl was admitted to an In-Patient unit near college, and I visited her regularly. Her family seemed to care little about her, and she emphasized that " she had nothing in common with her parents, and that they did not understand her." We received rather disquieting accounts from the Doctor who was looking after her. Mary's behaviour, after the first few days, seemed quite irresponsible. On one weekend leave from the unit, she returned from a visit to her family with two puppies, and I had the opportunity of meeting her father when he came over to fetch the dogs. He was a country solicitor, kindly and well meaning, but totally bewildered by his daughter's behaviour. He told me that her headmistress had informed him that Mary's intelligence was well over that needed for University entrance, but that she had refused to stay at school to take the necessary exams.

More than once over the next few weeks, Mary asked me rather despairingly " why do I do such stupid things? I don't really want to, at least I suppose I do at the time." Each of the " things " referred to was more foolish than the one before, and made her return to college more uncertain.

On discharge from the Unit she returned home, and almost at once stole a batch of prescription forms from her local G.P., by which she obtained a quantity of barbiturates which she proceeded to take on two occasions in public places, one on a railway station, and the other in a church. Of course, each time an ambulance was called and she found herself in hospital. After the second admission, another psychiatrist saw her in the General Ward of the hospital and advised the parents that she should be admitted to her local mental hospital for long-term treatment. To this, Mary agreed.

Up to this time, I had reassured her that, if she could co-operate with treatment and that the doctor in charge of the case would confirm that she was making progress, she would probably be able to resume her Course the following year. She had repeatedly asked for such reassurance, but had not been able to accept it. The hospital near her home was too far for me to visit, but I wrote to her, and she did not answer.

About eight months later, I had a letter from Mary saying that she had " been discharged, cured, from hospital, and had been advised to come back to college." The Principal wrote to the Superintendent of the hospital concerned, asking for confirmation, and found that the statement was completely untrue. Once again

Mary had been unable to co-operate with treatment, and had left after a few weeks against medical advice.

I have heard nothing since. Was there anything more I could have done? . . .

Obviously this record is no less a cry for help from the Tutor than from the girl, but this is a case when it was too late. A possible answer would seem to be early diagnosis of such a latent psychopathic condition in the remote hope that, caught in time, the seeds of normal development could be nurtured by understanding.

17

The Physically Handicapped

___

TO BE condemned to a lifetime of imprisonment for a crime that one did not commit—this, to many of us, must be the ultimate nightmare. But until recently this was the lifelong nightmare to which the sufferer from cerebral palsy was condemned. Like a wild bird caged and unable to get out, the mind of the sufferer was similarly restricted; and if that mind was a rare one, the mind of the gifted, the agony of the condition was that much intensified. In such a case, never was the word *gift* more of a misnomer.

The symptoms of this tragic brain affliction are such that the uncoordinated bodily movements and, as is often the case, varying perceptual deficiencies, were only too easily misinterpreted as indications of mental deficiency. Thus, a child whose movements seemed to bear no relation to his intentions and was also unable to communicate verbally was, ipso facto, an idiot; and who could be blamed for not seeing the quality that lay behind the flapping arms, kicking legs and incoherent speech?

It is not much more than a quarter of a century since we have been able to separate in our minds the outward appearance of cerebral palsy from possible inward brilliance. True enough, the condition *can* impair innate intelligence, but primarily this is due to the agony of attempting to relate bodily movement to bodily need, or verbalization to that which needs to be said when all is against succeeding in the attempt. The most basic actions in anyone uninstructed in the ways of making their crippling condition less burdensome produces a degree of frustration which leaves little time or energy to employ intelligence.

Cerebral palsy covers a group of disabilities, the basic common factor to all being damage to the parts of the brain which control movement, hearing and sight. There are difficulties of hearing and sight, of feeling and perception (the inability to distinguish between a circle and a square) which may be death to the possibility of achieving any mathematical skill, and at the same time there may be a gift for language and the graphic use of words. On the other hand, intelligence may be high yet communication negligible because of the inability to speak clearly.

Movements are uncoordinated; the sufferer, trying to pick something up from a table, may sweep it on the floor. Yet the attempt to control these wild movements, to " make an effort," only exacerbates the condition and an even greater display of uncontrollable frenzy is the result.

Cerebral palsy takes several forms. That described above is known as " athetoid," and it is among this group that one is most likely to find the highly intelligent victims. Here the damage to the brain is deep-seated and thought to occur in the basal ganglia, as opposed to the " true " spastic, whose brain damage occurs elsewhere.

The " true " spastic suffers from brain damage in the cerebral cortex. The main symptoms are stiffness and weakness of the muscles affecting one or other limb. Thus, if the arm and leg on one side of the body are affected, he will be called " hemiplegic." If only the legs, a " paraplegic," and if only one arm or leg, a " monoplegic."

There is a third group suffering from damage to the cerebellum, which is manifested by a general unsteadiness. But members of all three groups are commonly referred to as " spastics " although it is only the second group which qualifies for the use of the term in a strictly clinical sense.

To the layman the easiest way to understand the condition is to consider the brain as a highly complex telephone switchboard into which messages (calls) are constantly arriving from outside, the calls made, so to speak, by the senses reacting to an observation. These messages amount to a request for appropriate action (the many actions involved, for instance, in merely turning over the page of a book, the movement of the arm, the pressing of the page by a finger and so on). Unfortunately, the message is plugged through to the wrong department, and the wrong information is given. Thus the bodily movements, in answer to the simple need to turn over the page of a book, resemble more the actions of someone in the throes of a minor fit.

Every six hours, throughout Britain, a spastic child is born and, for the time being, because there is no known cure we can do no more than try to make their lot easier. Naturally the earlier the diagnosis the better, for then a plan can be made for treatment and general life situations (including schooling). As a result, the child will be given the chance to improve by coming to terms with his condition, rather than worsen through frustration and the emotional disturbances that lie in frustration's wake.

The authors are concerned, however, only with those children who, for all their tragic functional disability, are ironically gifted with high intelligence. It is with a sense of relief that one is able, at last, to consider an educational outlet for such children, a re-markable Grammar School near Tonbridge in Kent, a school in which the only " normal " people are the teachers, for the entire body of pupils are spastic.

The Delarue School is the first Grammar School in the world to be opened for the education of spastic children. It is housed in a modern well-designed building (completed early in 1964) placed around grass courtyards and looks no different from an ordinary school, but very different from the conventional idea of an institution for cripples.

Nevertheless, the school *is* different in many remarkable ways. It is purpose-built and the classrooms, all on the ground floor, are connected by unusually wide corridors, for they are the roadway down which children can move in their wheelchairs. Doors are wider than usual and the handles set low, so that those in chairs can open them easily.

Apart from the normal curriculum, independence is learned here and is considered just as important as mathematics. One day these tragically afflicted young people will have to make their own way in the world.

At the main entrance concrete ramps make it easy for the chairs to be unloaded, and from then on the children are on their own, to wheel down the corridors and into the classrooms where they take their places at their own desks (specially designed in the form of an E with the middle bar missing, so the wheelchair can fit in and the student have easy access to his books all round him, in formica-covered wells).

Everywhere can be seen calculating machines, and on many desks an electric typewriter, for at Delarue every modern aid is available to help the student cope with his work. Sometimes hand movement is so unpredictable that the keyboard has to be covered with a piece of metal with holes for the letters, through which it is possible for a piece of stick to be jabbed by one good hand. Through such a primitive method lies the possibility of a new facility. But the children here have a zest for learning that makes them a joy to teach.

Delarue School opened in 1955 and two years later it was officially recognized by the Ministry of Education who publicly congratulated the National Spastics Society on the way they had accommodated, equipped and staffed the school. "They have attracted an efficient staff and provided a place to which parents must be proud to send their sons and daughters, and which these severely handicapped pupils must be proud to attend."

The original headmaster was not only an outstanding teacher but also an outstanding administrator, never ceasing to press for new buildings and better staff conditions. He insisted that pupils be instructed in Art and Handicrafts, for he knew that, for the handicapped, the use of the hands for an activity such as needle-work, helps a girl control her movements and this, in turn, makes her more acceptable to an intolerant world.

As in any good school the students do not keep rigidly to "form" for Maths and English, but work in sets according to intelligence and, to a certain extent, according to the degree of disability. The real grouping depends upon the extent of physical handicap, for like the students at the various schools for creatives, they lead a double life. Time must be found for them to have physiotherapy, frequent medical check ups, visits to the dentist (teeth often need extra special care) and so on. Everything in the life of a spastic child takes so much longer to accomplish. Getting up in the morning, washing, brushing teeth, combing hair, even eating breakfast are almost as energy-consuming as a full day's work for a normal child. But lessons still have to be done and this means wrestling with the very mechanics of reading and writing. Somehow, with the courage that has brought them so far, the children manage.

For those who cannot write at all, amanuenses are employed. Usually these " right arms " live locally and work with one child for at least a term, and during this term learn to identify with the child's particular problems. One such amanuensis, in order to assist a brilliant pupil in her studies of Greek and Hebrew at Advanced Level, learned the alphabet of these languages, so that she could take down the work at the student's dictation!

Children come to Delarue from all over the country. They are seen by an assessment panel at the Spastics Society's headquarters near Regent's Park in London. The panel consists of a Paediatrician, Educational Psychologist and social worker, so that the child is assessed to be fit enough physically and intellectually. At the same time the family situation is assessed, for this is most important. Many parents of handicapped children are so over-anxious about them that the children have hardly ever been allowed to do anything for themselves. And, of course, a busy mother with a severely disabled child finds it much easier to wash and dress him herself than to allow him even to do the things he is capable of doing by himself. At Delarue, for all the fact that such help continues to be available, it is not given unless absolutely necessary.

The present headmaster took over the school in 1964. His own twelve years old son is a spastic and so badly affected that he will never be able to benefit from the kind of education that his father's school can offer.

There are now eighty-five pupils (March 1965) all of whom, incidentally, are paid for by their local Education Authority, the exceptions being short term pupils from abroad, and in such cases the parents pay. Such an arrangement is made possible because, now and again, a regular pupil may have to enter hospital for some time, either for intensive treatment or for an operation.

The ratio of teachers to children is one to five and there is also a house-parent staff who care for the children out of school time, and the proportion of this staff to the children is about the same. Both teachers and house-parent staff are mixed, so that the pupils lead a normal life, meeting and being cared for by men and women. The attempt, indeed, of providing a background of " normality " is such that even the dormitories in the school buildings nevertheless are that much removed from the classrooms to give a pupil the feeling that he is " arriving " at school in the morning, like any other child.

The number confined to wheel chairs does not constitute more than a third of the total at any one time, otherwise the very complex arrangements for their care would break down completely.

At the moment of writing, some twelve children need every help with feeding, while others get minimal help in cutting up their food. All eat together, except those who are undergoing intensive instruction and they have their meals in the occupational therapy room and join the others later. Indeed, the occupational therapists at this school have an over-ridingly important function, and their job is very much more than the conventional idea of instruction in basket work for instance. They work closely with the doctors, always considering ways in which the pupils can become ever more independent of help, ever more capable of achieving tasks for themselves. As a result, unusually strong effective ties exist between pupil and therapists.

Children come to Delarue later than they would come to Grammar School, were they not handicapped, for time is of the essence to the spastic child. They have had to cram much unusual learning into their first few years, learning about their bodies and what they can and cannot make them do, learning that they are handicapped . . . different from others and even feared, occasionally, by others, learning indeed that no matter how intelligent, they can easily be considered moronic, learning ever that learning itself is going to be that much more of a trial for them than for their healthy contemporaries.

They are, thus, usually two years behind academically—and instead of starting Grammar School education at eleven, as they would in normal circumstances, they are at least twelve and a half by the time they arrive at Delarue.

All the children in the top form take some " O " level subjects, and ten to fifteen go on to the "A" level—a large proportion for a school of just over eighty pupils. Guidance for future careers is a question to which much thought is given. It is little use encouraging the pupils to read subjects at a University they cannot later enter. In fact much research still needs to be done into the potential employment of spastic children of high intelligence, and possibilities for entry into the professions should be constantly under review, so that ultimately there is no chance of creating a feeling of rejection —rejection by the very society which encouraged them to make such prodigious efforts to overcome their handicap in the first place.

There remains always the emotional factor, often an important consideration in the lives of the cerebrally palsied. Dr. Kenneth Soddy, the Consultant Psychiatrist, believes that the actual handicap plays only a minor part in the total disturbance, and of primary importance is the reaction of the parents to a severely handicapped child who cannot be cured. Thus, early diagnosis and follow-up visits by the social worker are essential. The more intelligent the child, the more he will feel frustrated, and the more agitated and anxious this makes him, the less he will be able to communicate. Acceptance in its widest sense is needed, together with infinite patience.

It is in such an atmosphere of loving tolerance and patience that the pupils of Delarue prosper to the limit of their tragically curtailed capabilities. They are encouraged to take part in outside activities, some sing in the local choir, one girl teaches at Sunday School, and they have their own scout troop, constantly in touch with other similar troops.

At weekends at least half the pupils go out on their own, sometimes to a film, perhaps to do some shopping in nearby Tonbridge. Theatre parties are organized, and football and cricket matches visited. A few of the older students have invalid cars, and get about in this way.

Naturally they cannot participate in most games that normal children play, but they do become involved in all the ones that are possible for them, such as chair football, and archery. There is a Bridge Club every Saturday, and Chess is very popular, even though the pieces may well have to be moved with the toes instead of by hand!

What is striking—one notices it immediately one sets foot in the school—is the tremendous care the pupils take with their appearance. The girls have advice on hair styling (which they can manage by themselves with just a little help), all the students are neatly dressed and allowed to show striking individual preferences.

Sexual difficulties do arise, occasionally, in the lives of these gifted handicapped youngsters, but the staff are trained to help them overcome such problems, and although boy or girl will be unhappy in the knowledge that it may not be possible for them to have the complete fulfilment they crave, their very fortitude enables them to formulate, unusually early, a philosophy of life. There is, indeed, a branch of Christian Union in the school and one can hear the age old problems of good and evil, guilt and punishment, being discussed by those very children who have, perhaps, had more than their fair share of "punishment." A punishment, it would seem, for being born at all.

18

The Maladjusted

PETER was just seventeen, and he had a problem . . . it was life itself. He was fair, tall for his age, a boy who could look directly at no-one, a boy who stooped as if the weight of the burden he carried was too much for his shoulders; for indeed it was.

His early days seemed uneventful because, by nature, he was quiet. But even then, there were difficulties. For instance, there seemed to be an inexplicable rift between himself and his Civil Service father.

This worthy man, fairly high up in the Service, wanted Peter to have, easily, the advantages that were denied *him* as a youngster. He wanted Peter to shine at college—as the boy should have done, because he was very clever. He gave his son generous pocket money, he wanted to encourage him to work well, to improve all the while. But somehow there was a lack of contact. They seemed to have nothing in common, but in all fairness to the father, Peter's difficulty in relating went far beyond the parental situation.

Why should he be like this? There seemed to be nothing wrong with his recently married brother. His young sister was already getting excited over her first dates, yet Peter seemed to want nothing that a " normal " boy would desire.

His mother, a fussily anxious woman, was inclined to smooth over his inadequacies, even though she worried at his marked lack of interest in such " healthy " objects as motor-bicycles and girl-friends. And when, finally, he took to bed, saying that he felt ill, and didn't want to get up at all, well, he was a growing boy, wasn't he? And growing boys needed rest.

But the family doctor didn't think so. He thought, in fact, that Peter should be seen by a psychiatrist.

At the hospital, Peter was tested for his intelligence. His I.Q. was 168, close to genius class. But this was not so surprising in a lad who, during his earlier schooldays, always had outstanding reports and had taught himself to read long before he ever attended school.

What had gone wrong with Peter? What conflict in his emotional life had damaged him, it would seem, irreparably? What emotional war had reduced him to apathy, made him finally indifferent to his school work, indifferent to punishment, indifferent to people even of his own age?

When Peter was interviewed, he seemed remote. There were long pauses as he talked, as if the very effort to communicate was too much for him. He said he would rather be dead, but it seemed (luckily) he could not raise the energy to consider ways of achieving this desire.

Everything was too much trouble. He had no contact with anyone. The future? Who wanted a future? There was nothing to attract him to make the slightest effort to stay alive. So why not go to bed and simply wait for nothingness. . . .?

Or an answer to an unstated cry for help? For someone to come to his aid? A place was found for Peter with a small group of high I.Q. maladjusted boys, but it was more than a year before he showed a spark of interest. Since then, there has been a slight improvement, but Peter is permanently scarred, and will never be able to exploit his potential brilliance.

Should anybody be blamed for Peter? Blame produces nothing, and weakens the need to be constructive. Perhaps the parents *were* to blame (" there is no such thing as a problem child, only problem parents ") but who was to blame for them? When did the chicken come, and when the egg?

There would seem to be only one effective method to halt a pattern of neurosis extending from parent to child and, in the case of the structurally weak and, therefore easily damaged child, the possibility of psychosis. It is the method of early diagnosis. Again and again, enlightened educationalists (such as Otto Shaw) emphasize the urgent need for this awareness of disturbance in the very young, so that they can be caught in time before the damage ingrows to such an extent that it becomes irreparable.

In extreme cases, such as that of Peter, the " patient " has to be removed from home because it is there, no matter how concealed in networks of self-deception, that the centre of disturbance lies. It is the very relationship which is to blame, a relationship gone bad. And like a rotten apple in the middle of healthier fruit, the damage can only spread and deepen.

The number of places in this country catering for the high I.Q. maladjusted child are few. Like any other institution, whether it be the House of Commons or a business enterprise, such an establishment will be as good as the people at the top, and take its tone from the person who is in charge, and this person must be an almost god-like mixture of compassion and firmness. Two such people come quickly to mind, Otto Shaw and George Lyward.

" Your son should be removed as soon as possible, both for his sake and for that of the school. We are quite unable to offer him what he needs at present." George Lyward has spent the last forty years of his life caring for boys between the ages of sixteen and twenty-one, many of whom have had such a reaction from headmasters finally unable to cope.

Underachievement by itself is bad enough, but when supplemented by compulsive stealing, lying, running away, hostility to all in authority, or total lack of interest in life, well, how long can the fondest parents deceive themselves? Sometimes they seek the help of a psychiatrist, or a probation officer—if it has come to that—but sooner or later, someone is bound to say . . . " what about George Lyward? "

Lyward is now in his sixties, a man of great charm, and the sort of personality which attracts devotees to his cause. After fifteen years of teaching, he had finally decided that his chief interest was with boys who could not fit into the school system, for even in those early and unenlightened days, he had realized that such problems originated in the failure to grow up emotionally as contrasted with others of the same age.

He felt then, as he does today, that the kind of help required could be given within a special community where, along with other boys, they could learn to live with themselves and each other, where each boy could be accepted as a person, but where lessons were not a matter of classroom routine, but organized as a specialized and individual need.

Lyward had a genius for friendly persuasion, and several doctors to whom he had talked saw, in his convictions, a possible solution to the waste of high intelligence due to emotional disturbance.

He and his wife had just taken a house in Kent called Guildables, and it was not long before two boys were sent to him in need of the sort of help he could give.

In 1935, Mr. and Mrs. Lyward moved to Finchden Manor where they have remained ever since, except for a few years during the War when they had to move, Finchden being on the direct route to London from the coast. The Army took over at short notice during the invasion scare.

After the War, the effect of unplanned evacuation and consequent separation from the parents quickly showed itself. Intelligent children had been taken from their families at a moment's notice, and often found themselves in village schools where the harassed teacher either did not realize their potential or was able to offer little individual help. This, in addition to the child being taken away from the parents, often paved the way for delinquent behaviour. The first boy to have Finchden Manor fees paid by the Local Authority arrived in 1944, and since then there has been an unending stream of applications.

Boys are referred by General Practitioners, Psychiatrists, Probation Officers, and other Social Workers. Up to two hundred boys a year have to be turned down, for the strengths and weaknesses of the whole group have to be considered when a new boy is admitted. The entire atmosphere of the community is altered by every new admission.

Parents in great distress of mind often turn up on the doorstep, begging for their boy to be admitted immediately. This is usually due to a final and complete breakdown in the communication between parent and son. Both feel guilty about the home situation, but neither is able to cope one minute longer.

Lyward will nearly always make time for an interview, however brief, and this will remove the tension, at any rate, temporarily. He will explain patiently about the waiting list, and ask for school and doctor's reports, so that the case can really be considered on its individual merits.

Getting a vacancy is always a major operation. Usually the social worker takes the boy down. As they drive into the courtyard, heads are poked through windows, a boy walking through the hall may give a friendly wave, a member of the staff comes to meet the boy, reports are handed over to Lyward, and the social worker goes off to have lunch in Rye, and a walk on the nearby marshes. This isolated part of Kent is haunted country, a place where miracles can happen, and at Finchden they quite often do.

On return the worker is shown up to the study, the power house of Finchden. By this time the boy has been seen by Lyward and other members of the staff and, of almost equal importance, by the other boys. He has had a chance to feel something of the atmosphere, and now the question is put to him—" would you like to come to Finchden? " If he asks to think it over, he is assured that he can write and give his answer when he has made up his mind. If he says no, this is also expected, though sometimes a desperate letter is received in a few days, begging for admission and showing, perhaps for the first time, that the child is prepared to ask for help. This may well be the first and one of the most difficult steps on his way back to health.

What are the other boys like? This, of course, is one of the first questions that parents ask. It is not enough to say that they look like any other group of boys at a country school. This is not true. The occasional rebel clumps around in jeans and boots, still in revolt against the system that rejected him even though his is a Public School background, because indeed, his *is* a Public School background. Then again, if the boy comes from an unconventional home, or through a Court, his insecurity may make him dress with excessive neatness. Either way it is accepted and gradually, as he settles down, clothes become more suited to the kind of life that he now lives.

Maladjustment is not like measles. It cannot be caught. Boys do not infect each other; each child's problem is unique to itself although each falls into general clinical groups. There are the boys whose reaction to stress is one of withdrawal. This may show itself in his being quite unable to leave the house, perhaps compelled to stay in bed, the only place where he feels safe. It does not indicate laziness. If roused and urged or nagged (for parents are human and have been told, perhaps, that there is nothing physically wrong, which is true) the child may either dissolve into tears, so inappropriate to the situation, or become hostile and accuse the parents of not understanding, which is also true, but neither does the boy understand.

Sometimes his illness gives rise to obsessional symptoms. We all have some of these—the housewife constantly compelled to straighten a picture which is no more than a fraction out of true; the executive whose ashtray must always be in a certain place on his desk, and so on. In an extreme case, a child so afflicted will, for instance, fold clothes in a certain way when going to bed, but they are never folded quite " right." So they have to be folded again, usually in a sequence of numbers, three, six, nine, until going to bed becomes agony and maybe prolonged until the early hours of the morning when, if the ritual is interrupted, there is a feeling that something terrible will happen. Such a condition must, of course, be treated, for the child cannot be contained in an ordinary school, but once the acute phase has passed, time has been lost, lessons not learned, and the resultant stress may produce more anxiety and the return of the symptoms. Finchden is a place where these things are understood, where behaviour is not a matter of conforming to a certain code, and no-one says " that is not done here." This in itself gives a great sense of security to an acutely anxious boy.

Pilfering is common in small children, most of us have done it, but when this continues it is a sign of disturbance, and because we have in England set such a high value on property, we become very disturbed indeed about pilfering. It is considered highly anti-social, and in a boarding school, an insecure, unhappy, hostile boy may steal from his fellows. The things he steals fall into three groups; they are things which he would like to possess, a camera, a pair of field glasses, a transistor radio; the fact that he may have one of his own at the time, or that if asked, the parents would probably buy him one, does not really affect the issue. The things he steals may never be used. Indeed, they may be so distinctive, that he would find it impossible to brazen it out that the article was his, so they are hidden.

The next group of pilferers are those who steal money from a locked desk in the master's study, or from the pocket of a blazer in the cloakroom. When accused, the child will almost always try to deny it, although he may be confronted with undeniable proof. He will not react except by hostile silence, or a storm of aggressive tears to the invitation to " confess." It will probably emerge, however, that he has in fact been stealing for some considerable time before he is caught; that the money was spent in buying sweets or cigarettes which he then used, usually without success, as barter for friendship. In the third group, the stealing is done in such a way that the " crime " is bound to be found out. In fact, punishment seems to be what the child is inviting and when asked about it will nearly aways say: " What are you going to do now? " All three groups of juvenile thieves are met with by school masters who find them an almost insoluble problem within the normal educational framework. The parents are asked to remove the boy at short notice, all their hopes for his future crashing down, and the future seems black.

If the boy belongs to the third group, in the child with a high I.Q., it may be interpreted as a cry for help. In the low I.Q. child, pointless stealing may be symptomatic of a borderline defective who does not really know how else to get attention. The motive is the same in the gifted child, but it indicates a very great state of anxiety and a pressing need for skilled psychiatric help. The boy who has tried to buy friends with goods bought with stolen money is also in desperate need of help. He feels, and usually is, friendless, isolated from his fellows, and rejected by them because of his general attitude.

In the case of a child with high intelligence, the stealing episodes may be highly organized and planned. Satisfaction gained comes partly from the fact of " having put one over on the bastards," who thought that they could keep things away from him—as his parents kept their love from him, as perhaps he may feel.

Finchden has taken many boys from all three groups. Sometimes they have been unable to come to terms with their problem, even in that sympathetic atmosphere, but usually, after an initial stormy period presenting strain both for the other boys and the staff, the child begins to understand why he steals, and gradually begins to accept help without trying to grab for it.

At Finchden the therapy does not only come from Mr. Lyward and the members of his staff, it also comes from the other boys. People learn to live with themselves, and therefore with other people. Naturally, leaving the school presents many problems, and Lyward does not willingly let a boy leave until he is strong enough to do so. Afterwards, he can keep in touch by letter, and even come back for a weekend as a friend. Indeed this keeping in touch may go on for years after they have left. It gives a feeling of support, so that the chance of being overwhelmed by life when away from the school is not so great.

The staff at Finchden fill many different roles in the course of any one day. Father, brother, friend, counsellor, teacher, but always the person who can accept the boy as he really is without accepting everything he does. This kind of real acceptance is the basis of all treatment. A few of the teachers have been to Finchden as boys themselves, unorthodox by general educational standards, maybe, but here it works, for all are outstanding in some academic field, with additional insight due to having overcome their own early problems.

George Lyward is that rare thing, a completely dedicated man, interested only in helping boys whom a psychiatrist will call mal-adjusted, a magistrate call delinquent, and whom families call impossible. Mostly he has succeeded, but every boy who has been to Finchden has seen that here is a place where one can be healed, where one can grow up in an atmosphere of understanding and compassion.

Redhill School, also in Kent (a few miles beyond Maidstone), could be called the quintessence of Finchden inasmuch as all of its pupils are of the highest intelligence, some indeed beyond classification so acute is their intellect.

The Principal, Otto Shaw, is a remarkable man, a lay analyst himself and of an articulateness which made it preferable for the interview, granted to the authors, to be reproduced verbatim, as a series of questions and answers:

Q. What is Redhill School?

A. It is a registered charitable trust, recognized by the Ministry of Education for the education and psychological treatment of maladjusted boys of very superior intelligence. It is a boarding school, recognized as a Grammar School, and our children come roughly at the age of eleven. We don't like taking boys much over the age of fourteen, because by that time, certain of their habit patterns are set.

Q. Why do you only admit boys of very high I.Q.?

A. We didn't at first. Originally we opened because in those days boys were called delinquent or "problem." Indeed, sometimes no-one seemed to have a name for it at all, and we were taking on any child who obviously couldn't fit in with his home environment, or couldn't fit into an ordinary school. It was only round about 1944, with the passage of the '44 Education Act, that we decided to seek recognition as a Grammar School, for by that time we had, willy nilly, started attracting only very intelligent boys. Having been accepted as a Grammar School, we naturally concentrated on boys who were likely to fulfil the reasonable demands of, say, a fairly conventional Sixth form. As time went on and the excitement and pleasure of the work became more and more apparent, we then decided to concentrate on boys who were even of much higher intelligence than those usually found in the average Grammar School.

Q. In the early days, where did you find your finance from, in order to run the school?

A. Often from my own pocket! In those days, psychological treatment of children who were not behaving properly was a novelty, and in the first place it was rather difficult to make certain that local education authorities, Courts and probation officers really understood the purpose of psychological treatment. We had no difficulties with clinics; they understood, but in those days there were very few clinics and such as there were, were mainly concentrated in London and the Home Counties. Now, of course, with the dissemination of knowledge on this subject, we get applications to take cases from clinics, educational authorities in England and, surprisingly enough, some from Scotland. So, as you can imagine, there is no limit to the flood of applications. In fact, nowadays, we are getting sometimes as many as twenty applications a week. Out of these we would dearly love to take three or four who are extremely appropriate to our form of treatment, and whom we think we could benefit. But, unfortunately, we are limited because due to accommodation, we can only take about ten or twelve a year. It is unfortunate that a good many of those children do not receive treatment, and therefore must go through life permanently impaired.

Q. Do you think there should be more schools like your own?
A. Indeed I do. There is no doubt whatever that Society is really living in a terrible state of sin about its failure really to provide education for all these devient children. It's a sorry story, because the financial results of their failure are very expensive. It is far better, of course, to spend a little money in getting them cured, expensive as it may appear to be at the time, rather than wait until the cost of a cure, or the far greater costs of an inadequate personality, has to be accepted by the community for all time. As for similar schools, there are a number of highly reputable schools for maladjusted children, but unfortunately only one establishment which specializes in Grammar School type children and in what others call geniuses, and those schools are doing excellent work. But there is still a vast field; one can judge from the fact that whenever one tries to seek a place for a maladjusted child in a school for such children, as I often do in my Court work, usually one discovers there is no vacancy, and I am afraid a waiting list is often quite meaningless. One day, perhaps, we

shall get over staffing difficulties because that is a very real problem in running a school for maladjusted children—and really do the job properly. But when we reach that stage, we shall be well on the way to emptying the prisons and the mental hospitals.

Q. Do you think that schools for maladjusted children should be divided between those catering for children of normal intelligence, and those like your own school, catering for children of superior intelligence?

A. It should be possible for children to meet in parity, although their attainments and attributes vary to a great extent. I don't think there's any particular need to train teachers in some specialist manner to cope with very gifted children. In some of our ordinary Grammar Schools, and in some Public Schools, there are geniuses, and there's no reason to think that a teacher would fail to accept the challenge. The doubt comes, rather, where a child who is of very high intelligence has obviously failed to show the equivalent of attainment which one would expect from someone of that high order of intelligence. And there, I suppose, either to some extent, the teachers fail—although I feel we should be reluctant to apportion blame—or else the child's own personal involvement is, perhaps, of a neurotic kind, or perhaps of an unstable kind, and thus prevents him from really showing the genius or the qualities of mind that his other attributes would suggest.

Q. Manifestations of emotional disturbance must be apparent from very early years. I believe that the majority of teachers, either from impatience or sheer lack of time in too large classes, prefer to ignore such manifestations. Do you think there should be training, both for teachers and headmasters, to recognize psychological disturbance in a child at a time when, with proper treatment, he or she can develop out of this condition?

A. I think you are being rather charitable in the reason you give for a teacher failing to recognize an infantile symptom at a Primary School stage. I feel that probably the reason is sheer ignorance. In Kent there is a psychiatrist who is a man of considerable foresight, great imagination and, furthermore, who can take the trouble to follow up his cases year by year. He has been to some pains in going round to the Primary Schools and explaining to teachers what he believes to be the need for early diagnosis. So, if one finds a little child a little bit weepy, a little bit disconsolate but, at the same time, who is wetting his pants to the extent that a teacher could observe a small puddle under the desk, that is not a symptom that should escape notice and receive no more than some flatulent remark to the effect that " he'll grow out of it." Maybe he will grow out of it, but growing out of a symptom of that kind most certainly means that the child is growing into a symptom of an even more difficult kind which will be more delayed in its cure, or amenability to a cure, because it is a replacement of a more primary symptom.

Frequently, a child wetting itself at school is merely asking a way, which he knows is appropriate, for Mummy to come and take him home. Just as we, when we first wet our napkins, always found that Mummy rushed up to attend to us, so the little child, bereft (he feels) of his mother by going to the school for the first time, will return to that early call. Now, the teacher who is wise will interpret that as a call for Mummy and try to provide that maternal affection, maternal care and maternal solicitude which that child needs. If it is as superficial as that, the wetting will stop. Frequently, however, it is a far deeper thing which did not have its springs from being made to go to school, but really had its cause from within the family. In such cases, one can only hope that the queues for child guidance treatment will diminish, and they can only diminish by the provision of more child guidance clinics as envisaged in the Underwood Report, and then the teacher will feel that the Clinic is a valuable instrument in his, the teacher's, total care of the child. It is utterly ridiculous to wait until there is some delinquent symptom or some sexual symptom when the boy is about twelve or thirteen. Only the other day, I met a couple of quite small boys who had set light to a barn . . . they were charged in my juvenile court. It is very difficult to find a solution to that outside of psychological treatment, but going into the matter, one saw all kinds of early symptoms, sometimes only suggested, sometimes fully acted out, which, had they been recognized at the time when they first appeared, would have prevented this act of delinquency, and would have enabled the child to understand that what he was doing sprang from the home situation, and perhaps he would have chosen a happier means of expressing himself.

When we have really grasped the need for early diagnosis of difficulties of behaviour, when we really have tried to grasp the need to understand why a child is not revealing his very high order of ability, then, of course, we shall go further to shortening the queues, not only for the clinics, but for the mental hospitals as well.

Q.   What is the proportion of successful cures amongst the boys at Redhill School?

A.   We have been very fortunate. Perhaps it would be unfair to claim credit for our good work, because we choose cases. We choose children we genuinely think we can help. So it would be rather surprising if it turned out that they didn't change for the better when we helped them. In effect, we have a negligible amount of failures. And the failures we have would not be recognized as failures by other people. Our criteria of success is not that they must show academic success—that's easy enough—but for them to make a good marriage. So if you ask me how we can tell whether a child is cured, I will say it is quite easy. We watch them marry, and then watch the way their children turn out. If the children are all right—then the original patient is cured! But this test is a severe one, and by anyone else's standards, our proportion of success is one hundred percent. On our own test, we have, perhaps, a ten percent. failure.

Q. Assuming that, one day we hope, the need to "spot" emotional disturbance will be fully accepted, do you think there should be a kind of psychiatrical liaison worker between school and parent?

A. There is certainly a case for providing a social welfare worker, or a psychiatric social worker for doing therapeutic work with parents. Of course, that work would not be called that, and the line to parents would be simply what the school was doing on behalf of their child . . . but it would, really, be therapeutic work on the parents. We do a great deal of that, although we do not call the people engaged on this work social workers. In fact, most of my colleagues can and do this work. But on the question of such liaison as you mention, if the staff of a school cannot do their own work without having to rely upon props or struts some other expert gives them, then they are not worth employment upon that particular job. They might be good at another job, for they are people of integrity and purpose. But there's no reason to think the job can be better done by having a proliferation of so-called psychiatric advice.

We must deny the need, however, that in all the social situations, the classroom situations, play and work situations, that a member of the staff should actively give analytical interpretations. That would lack taste . . . and wouldn't produce anything. The analytic work is done under the seal of professional secrecy and is done in absolute privacy. On the other hand, we have to be knowledgeable people, and if that knowledge is combined with a certain amount of compassion and charity, again of a non-sentimental variety, that's all you want. All you want, indeed, but difficult enough to find.

Q. How do you select teachers for the school?

A. Above all, we choose men and women who are capable in themselves of leading a full and mature life, not people

who are always wistfully looking back to their own childhood, and trying to relieve part of it, partly at the expense,
but always through the children in their charge. So we avoid
those. We don't ask for any high-flyers, we ask for people
who are prepared to plod, prepared to work, prepared to
give, and prepared to understand. Such attributes, perhaps
over-angelic in many respects, do not come through
learning. They come through experience. Sometimes they
come at middle age or late in life, sometimes in the early
twenties. Whoever we appoint, and they have got to be
real colleagues, to identify themselves with our purpose,
we make certain that they are psychologically mature.

In work with maladjusted children it is necessary to break down
artificial barriers between adults and pupils. No-one who can
remember his own schooldays at all can have much doubt that
even under the most favourable circumstances, such barriers do
exist in the normal course of education. Teachers are a class
apart from pupils, with a different status, and working to a system
which requires them to maintain that separate status.

It is not easy for a pupil, particularly if maladjusted, to give
confidence to a member of a different group, and not easy for the
teacher to seek out such confidences. Such a system can work well
enough up to a point, and quite good superficial contacts can be
made where teaching is a matter of imparting knowledge, and will
even allow some teachers to exert a general influence on the ways
and habits of pupils. But it is easy for a teacher vastly to overrate
his moral influence, and to be deplorably ignorant of what pupils
think of his efforts. Where, as in the case of Redhill School, it is
urgently necessary to help a pupil to remould habits and qualities,
sometimes to a very deep level, it is a different matter. A different
system is needed. Hence self-government, the very basis of the
work of this remarkable school.

Instead of obeying all the orders, the pupils make some of the
decisions, and have greater freedom to criticise existing arrangements and to suggest new schemes. Meanwhile, the inner meaning,
the consideration which demands such self-government whatever

other merits it does or does not have, is this matter of closer personal relations between adults and pupils.

Many maladjusted children are antagonistic to adult dominance, others are suspicious of adults. Maladjustment starts at home, and difficult parents have set up in the child's mind images of adult life and purposes which now stand in the way of mutual confidence, even when (as in fact often happens) the teacher is not made a direct substitute for parents, and thus drawn directly into the child's inner conflicts.

But unless such barriers are broken, not only will the staff of the school be unable to give any adequate guidance, but also the insecurity, which lies at the roots of the pupil's maladjustment and which is, essentially, a reaction to parents and hence to adult figures in general, will be perpetuated, and it is hard to see how any genuine progress can be made. The object of self-government is to place adults in a new and different relationship to pupils which will make it harder for them to be set down, ex hypothesi, as members of a different group with alien aims and intentions, therefore easier for them to make their mark as individuals and individual personalities.

In Redhill its central function is the school meeting which, in its earliest form, was essentially a kind of enlarged family council, in which the adults present did not lay down the law, but showed the reasons for their opinions, and in which the opinions of pupils were also heard and treated with respect. The object was to demonstrate that adults present were not an alien, aggressive and dangerous group, but reasonable and co-operative.

After a period of trial and error, internecine conflict between contemporaries was separated from the over-all school meeting—a group of pupils, sitting as a bench of magistrates, could hear and decide charges. This involved selecting a sub-group of the more responsible pupils, with the title of Bench Members, from whom a panel could be selected to run any court. The proviso that in case of inability to decide, the Bench may take a public vote, was an additional safeguard which, it so happens, remains practically unused. Meanwhile, minor issues and small personal charges, which are often of great emotional significance to those who bring them, are dealt with quickly and concisely.

Bench Members carry out what would normally be considered prefectorial functions, but as agents of the " community " and with the good-will of the " community." They have no authority over other pupils which they can use for personal advantage, and they are best defined as pupils whose own behaviour has reached a relatively high level of personal responsibility, and who take an active and realistic interest in the welfare of the " community " and its individual members. Various methods of selecting Bench Members have been tried, but these are merely variations on a theme, for it is clear that no pupil will prove satisfactory as a Bench Member, or hold his position, unless he is acceptable (a) to staff, (b) to other Bench Members and (c) to the " community " as a whole.

The school meeting itself now revolves around a number of committees, elected twice yearly, whose chairman reports to the meeting on their activities and projects.

These are the :

> Food and Hygiene Committee.
> Sports Committee.
> Social Committee.
> Library Committee.
> Archives Committee.
> Exterior Maintenance Committee.
> Decorations Committee.
> Hobbies Council.
> Finance Committees.

Apart from any questions of the relationship between adults and pupils, self-government does in fact give more responsibility and more power of decision to pupils. This is necessary, for it is useless to bring a pupil to a point at which he can feel that old habits and modes of action were wrong, unless he can also be in a position to practise new ones. One meaning of committee work and bench membership is that the individual pupil is being provided with ways of testing newer and better social attitudes and even personal attitudes.

If, however, self-government is to serve therapeutic ends, there must evidently be a close and very effective control of its machinery by the staff. Control by pupils might serve many practical ends, might be both sensible and equitable, but it could never take into account the personal needs of an individual pupil from a therapeutic point of view. Each individual must be watched, encouraged to step forward as far as he can, and, at the same time, dissuaded (rather than forcibly prevented) from taking on responsibilities for which he is not yet ready. The social progress of the maladjusted leads along a narrow path between inertia on the one hand and difficulties and discouragement on the other. The staff must have, therefore, such hold, as personalities, on the machinery of self-government that they can ensure correct decisions are reached without appealing to superior status. At the same time, it is essential to the entire system that wherever pupils can be left to reach their own decision on grounds that the result, whatever it may be, cannot be seriously dangerous or inconvenient, then adults should stand aside. After all, the staff of Redhill School have no personal axe to grind. They are working for the potential happiness of their emotionally hurt charges.

CASE HISTORY (2)

Malcolm was born to two loving parents. He was an only child and he was starting to grow up and all was comely and wholesome. When he was five there was a dreadful tragedy.

When one reads about a fatal motoring accident in the newspapers, one cannot appreciate the depth of horror and pathos behind the report, and this accident resulted in the death of the boy's parents.

But Malcolm was lucky. He went to stay with an uncle and aunt, and there was every hope that he would be integrated among their family, and mix with his cousins quite happily.

Unfortunately, the uncle and aunt fell out . . . and this led to divorce. And so once again, Malcolm was bereft of parents. Twice this blow had struck him, once by death and once by divorce, so there is very little surprise that his own behaviour with other people, with teachers, with adults in general, with friends . . . and above all, with authority, became very disturbed. He did learn, too (and it was a most unfortunate lesson) that if he turned on the tap of sentiment, pulled out the stops of pathos, then other people would listen to him and tell him how sorry they were for him, and smother him with a kind of useless regard which could do very little to sort out his basic deprivation.

The first time Malcolm came to the attention of Redhill was when he had been caught breaking into other people's houses. Needless to say, he could do nothing in class. Malcolm's I.Q. level was that of genius, yet all he could do was aimlessly fiddle with ruler or compass, flick pellets at other people and, when rebuked, be very offensive to the teacher. He would go round, too, asking all kinds of questions. Indeed, talking to him sometimes was like reading " The Times " in a heavy gale. One would be overwhelmed, deluged, with question after question, and he'd never wait for the answer.

Basically and fundamentally, of course, Malcolm was asking a question which he could never really put into words . . . without it being cloyed by all sorts of extraneous attempts to catch sympathy . . . " Why did my parents die? Why did my next Mummy and Daddy fall out of love with each other? Please answer that question, please . . ." It was the question basic to all his needs.

Naturally, in a sympathetic atmosphere, the immediate delinquency mellowed, almost disappeared, but the problem was still there and had to be expressed. He wasn't punished for his thefts, he didn't receive dull, moral, sterile lectures asking him not to misbehave, but he received absolute tolerance which, in the case of such anti-social acts as the boy was still forced to perform, was very difficult, bearing in mind there was always the possibility that the boy was misinterpreting the true object of the toleration. Had he found a bunch of suckers who would put up with anything?

If this had been the case, nothing therapeutic would have been of any use. It was necessary to show him that one deplored what he did at all times, but didn't deplore *him*. One had to rebuke the sin, but not the sinner.

And, at last, he grasped the dichotomy. He produced fact after fact, thought after thought, feeling after feeling about the double parental deprivation. Gradually, he was brought to understand what he really looked for, and that no amount of breaking in, as it were, into Mummy's cupboard, in the form of a neighbour's house, could supply his basic need. No amount of angry questioning without waiting for the answer could ever provide a reason for the terrible trick that Fate had twice played upon him.

And when he did, at last, understand what he was doing, and why, Malcolm was able to form relationships within the school, realizing that charity and compassion wasn't given to him as a kind of inverted bribe, but because his need was realized. He ceased making demands in the extravagant arrant way he had learnt, and made legitimate demands, used the gift of his intelligence happily and firmly, and thus gradually came to terms with himself. Malcolm had started to grow up at last . . .

19

The Decompression Experiment

IT is yet another paradox of nature that the process of birth, the very creation of a new life, is fraught with danger, both to mother and to newly-born child. There is, also, a growing belief that as a result of the placenta's deterioration, during the last few months of pregnancy, other than in exceptional cases a mark occurs—a brain trauma—so infinitesimal that so far no instrument exists sensitive enough to reveal the injury. The condition is generally referred to as minimal brain damage, and the theory (well supported by a growing body of empirical discovery) is that we are all victims of such injury. Those of us, that is, who enjoy the full conventional period of gestation.

Now, the advantage of a nine months' period of gestation is that the physical potential of the newly-born child is assured, whereas premature babies are believed to be the inheritors of a weak constitution. The disadvantage, it would seem, is this minimal brain damage, a result of the life-giving placenta's deterioration.

The disadvantage of premature birth is, as mentioned, the predisposition towards physical weakness. But the advantage would seem to be a brain that is undamaged.

According to the innovators of decompression, it is the cells, or neurones, of the brain that suffer from the failure of the placenta to do its job for the full period of gestation, and when we realize that even the shortest coma, in an adult, produces some degree of cerebral damage, it is very understandable that a three months' failure of healthy blood supply to the embryo child is bound to have an incalculable effect on the healthy growth of the brain.

The answer would seem to be for a baby to be born with (a) the cerebral advantages of premature birth and (b) the sheerly physical advantages obtained from mature birth. This is no longer a dream, and the results are there for all to see.

Decompression is a method of indirectly introducing oxygen into the blood stream of pregnant women, and a special machine has been invented to make this possible. During recent years, much thought has gone into the question of keeping the mother healthy during pregnancy. She is urged to attend ante-natal clinics, to add milk and vitamins to her diet and to have her teeth attended to so that the baby, in his turn, should grow under the best possible conditions. But the results of decompression would suggest that this is not enough, for out of more than five thousand babies born of mothers who have received decompression, there has not, so far (1965) been *one single spastic*. In England and Wales, for instance, one child in every six hundred is a spastic. Thus, in what can be described as ideal circumstances, with all the medical advantages obtainable through the Welfare State, ten spastics will be born out of six thousand children. For none at all to be born out of 5,000 delivered of mothers who have received decompression, is an indication of the potential miracles such treatment seems capable of achieving. And, already, there would seem to be even greater ones, in the realms of early maturity.

If the soil of a garden is to produce healthy plants, it must be well nourished. In the case of the human seed, such nourishment is provided by a healthy flow of oxygenated blood into the placenta, via tiny twisting vessels called spiral artericles. All the growing cells in the embryo need this oxygen, and it is the blood cells in the brain which are most easily and quickly affected by lack of oxygen. It is they which are so important for the development of the whole child.

During the last two months of pregnancy, when the body of the mother is getting ready to expel the baby, the placenta begins to shrink, as its task is nearly over. It is during this time, according to the views of the man behind the decompression experiment, that damage to the brain cells of the baby is most likely to occur. Because of the degeneration of the placenta, the blood flow to the brain of the embryo is apt to slow down. Even more important, the spiral artericles are having to do extra work, because although the placenta has stopped growing and begun to shrink in preparation for its own expulsion, the baby has yet to double its size, and the tiny blood vessels through which the vital oxygenated blood flows can easily become clogged with sediment.

It was in May 1954 that Dr. O. S. Heyns, Professor of Obstetrics and Gynaecology at the University of the Witwatersrand, Johannesburg, who is also Chief Obstetrician and Gynaecologist for Johannesburg hospitals, made a striking discovery. With a colleague he was endeavouring to make a cinematograph record of the abdominal outline of a pregnant woman suffering excessive pain and with the possibility of giving birth to a dead or, at least, badly damaged child. Certain drugs were administered whose action, normally, relieved uterine contractions, thus, at the same time, making birth a failure. In this instance, the pain was diminished, but the contractions continued, and the period of unequivocal labour was, remarkably, no more than six hours.

A few weeks later, a similar experiment was enabled to be carried out and, as a result of this and further experiments, insight was obtained into the beneficial effects of abdominal muscular stretching, with the result that not only was the actual process of birth shortened to an astonishing degree, but the freshness and cheerfulness of the mother, prior to the birth, was outstanding.

Ultimately, to attain the necessary inflation of the abdomen by less dubious means than drugs, the idea of decompression occurred and, even later, a small chamber was built which could fit over the abdominal walls, and which incorporated a pump capable of introducing revitalizing oxygen into the system of the pregnant woman, through the use of artificially created muscular control. In two cases, babies were born less than three hours after the very beginning of labour.

This alone was remarkable, and was the beginning of many years of experiment, culminating in the establishment of the method to such an extent, that its use spread far beyond South Africa and, in London, the University College Hospital, at present, is treating certain expectant mothers in this way.

The Heyns Decompression Apparatus consists of a vacuum pump for extracting air from a chamber covering the abdomen.

In order to make sure the whole thing is airtight, the subject wears a plastic suit. By means of a valve under her finger-tip control, the air pressure is reduced inside the chamber. If she removes her thumb, the pressure returns to normal. When the pressure is reduced, the newly oxygenated blood from her lungs will flow more quickly to the area where pressure is lowest, the placenta will be filled with this pure blood, and the tiny spiral artericles will be flushed out. When the mother removes her thumb from the valve, the ordinary blood flow is restored and the blood in the placental pond, from which the baby receives his nourishment, flows away into the mother's blood stream as usual, to be re-oxygenated and start its journey all over again.

In appearance the apparatus seems to be clumsy. This is partly due to the fact that a woman in the final stages of pregnancy is not blessed with a sylph-like figure, but also because she is seated on a specially designed chair, onto which is fitted a backing plate. This backing plate has grooves at the side into which fits the fibre-glass tunnel which covers her abdomen, and from the edges of this, the plastic suit extends. In use it is perfectly comfortable, no pain is felt at any stage and during the daily half hour in the decompression suit (which Professor Heyns thinks should be used for the last eight weeks of pregnancy) the mother feels at ease, well, relaxed and with marked relief, also, from that miserable backache.

The apparatus is also used during the first stage of delivery. The idea behind this is that if the confinement is without complications the baby is likely to be more healthy and, as we have said, if his journey is an easy one, he arrives less distressed and with all his brain cells intact. So it is of vital importance that during the contractions which take place to speed the child on his way, the oxygen supply is not cut off. During the contractions of the uterus, however, the change in its shape brings it up against the very powerful rectus muscle and especially if the mother is tense or nervous, this muscle also tenses up. Therefore, not only does she experience further pain, but the passage of the baby is impeded, and the mother over-tires herself because of the unnecessary energy she is expending.

When the decompression apparatus is used during the first stage of labour the abdominal wall containing the rectus muscle is gently pulled up, out of the way, so that the change in the shape of the uterus is not interfered with. Pain is therefore relieved, and all the force of the contractions can be used to speed the baby on his way. As the mother does not tire so easily, and as she is not wasting energy, the baby moves easily into the best position for the actual birth.

Professor Heyns feels that the apparatus is only needed during the long first stage of the confinement. When the child actually starts to be born, the much shorter second stage starts, the mother is taken out of the apparatus from which she has derived much comfort, and the confinement proceeds in the conventional way. But it has been noted that this second stage is often much easier and considerably shorter than usual. The third stage, of course, is marked only by the expulsion of the placenta from which the baby has been nourished during the entire period of gestation.

It must be emphasized that at no time is oxygen pumped into any part of the mother. The apparatus merely ensures that when used during the last two months of pregnancy for about half an hour a day, those vital two months when the placenta is slowly deteriorating and a consequent failure of oxygenated blood begins, that newly oxygenated blood is enabled to flow more quickly and easily into the placental pool where it can prevent stagnation, and clear the blood vessels, from which the baby is being fed, of any sediment. This ensures that all the cells are well nourished, including those vital brain cells in the fast growing, but still embryo, brain. But anything that can relieve the general malaise of childbirth experienced by most mothers, is more than welcome.

This, then, is a description of the way in which the Decompression apparatus is used, but because the children born in this way are undamaged, there are far wider implications. It is well known that babies born as a result of a Caesarian operation are also undamaged by birth injury, but equally, this method could not be used in every case. Indeed, it is only undertaken when the doctor considers that the mother could not give birth in the ordinary way, because of some malformation. The other group of babies who arrive comparatively undamaged are those born prematurely. But here, as we have said, they are up against the sheerly physical loss entailed in such a birth. Before they can even begin to develop their intelligence, they have to make up for a physical development which should have occurred before they were born.

Before we consider the results of decompression, and they would seem to be remarkable, it might be as well to consider a completely different but related field. The field of brilliance, both past and present, and the, perhaps, astonishing realization occurs that brilliance and high achievement would seem, in many cases, to go hand in hand with a premature birth! If this is indeed the case, the beliefs of Dr. Heyns and his followers will be seen to be something more than the way-out thoughts of an imaginative group of people, with nothing to support these beliefs other than some incredibly precocious behaviour in some very young children born of mothers who gave birth to them with the assistance of decompression.

It is a popular misconception that child geniuses are weakly, and tend to die young. But it could be that, through mishandling and an over-emphasis on the sensational development of their gifts, that they were, literally, pushed into an early grave? (In a later chapter, we will discuss this common tendency to " push " a gifted child.)

Consider the case of Christian Heinrich Heinkin, perhaps the most celebrated child genius of all. His father, when Heinrich was only ten months old, is said to have realized that here was a child different from the rest, and a tutor was engaged for him. At this age he could name objects from pictures and two months later could remember stories from the Pentateuch. At the age of fourteen months, he could memorize parts from both the New and Old Testaments. By the age of four, he could read German, knew French, and could repeat fifteen hundred " sayings " in Latin.

Unfortunately, Heinrich wouldn't eat, but he would hardly seem to have had time to do so! A sickly child (the heritage of premature birth?), he was simply not given the opportunity to *be* a child, and even the granting of an audience by King Frederick IV would hardly seem to be a consolation for what can only be considered an outrageous and prolonged attempt to exploit his early gifts. His promise was never fulfilled . . . Heinrich was less than five years old when he died.

Sir Isaac Newton is known to have been a premature baby—his mother suffered from an irritable uterus. Voltaire, also, was known to be prematurely born, as was Winston Churchill (but in the latter case, the eugenesists would also put in a strong claim for the hereditary factor, for one of his ancestors was Elizabeth Tuttle, who is described as a woman " of great beauty, tall and distinguished in stature . . . of strong will, extreme intellectual vigour, of mental grasp akin to rapacity . . . attracting many by her charm "). In Churchill's family there are many people of outstanding intellectual and general ability, but he himself was in a class of his own, inasmuch as he evinced all the characteristics of premature birth relating to below-average achievement in early days. It was not until well into his young manhood that Winston Churchill's exceptional abilities began to manifest themselves. One could say that he took longer than most who were prematurely born to make up for the deficiencies of such a birth, in order that he might later develop intellectual powers of an unusual scale!

It is tempting to speculate whether other men of genius—who, like Pasteur, Hume and Goldsmith in addition to Newton and Churchill—were also premature babies, and that once they had overcome the physical handicaps caused by their low birth weight, the fact that they had suffered minimal, if any, neutronal damage enabled them to make full use of their gifts in diverse directions.

It would seem that the time is now ripe for intensive research into the birth conditions of famous and brilliant men. Perhaps we shall be astonished to learn that, in the case of so many, they, like Voltaire, were premature babies, unhampered in their intellectual development by the minimal brain damage which would seem to occur in those not born prematurely.

It is with such a rationale in mind that the decompression experiment can be seen as being of such potential significance. It is, of course, still in its infancy, but at the date of writing, the proportion of exceptionally advanced children is notably high.

In the last information to be revealed (the mothers from both black and white races) the following babies were analysed :

(a) 60 control babies from the Queen Victoria Hospital.

(b) 20 Bantu control infants from Moroka Township.

(c) 196 babies (known as the ANC series) whose mothers had up to 30 decompression runs during pregnancy.

(d) The Sanctuary Series of 30 babies whose mothers were unmarried and lived in a Home during their pregnancy.

(e) A Bantu group of 16 mothers who were given daily decompression during their last two months of pregnancy.

The ANC mothers were all attending the ante-natal clinic at the Queen Victoria Hospital, but they volunteered for ante-natal decompression and took great interest in their subsequent experiences, so in some ways they form a selected group. The Sanctuary girls were selected as they entered the Home, and one mother, at least, is known to be a mental defective with an I.Q. of only 55. The Bantu women were selected because it was thought by the doctors concerned that they would be temperamentally suited, being able as they were to attend their local clinic daily. It was felt that it was unreasonable to expect most of the women to attend hospital daily during the last few weeks so, where possible, apparatus was installed in the home.

The children were tested in accordance with already established findings that for each month of age, there is a norm for motor development, language, adaptive behaviour and social behaviour. These findings are based on results from experiments in the U.S.A. in which, over various months, 100 babies were regularly tested. True enough, by using this scale and, at the same time, saving an enormous amount of work involved in the formation of a new basis for comparison, differences of culture patterns between Bantu and white American babies had to be taken into consideration, but in all cases there were control babies for comparison.

The testing was carried out by three obstetricians, and ratings were obtained by dividing the development age by the chronological age. The motor and behaviour development were assessed together.

Babies were tested at all ages up to 24 months, and on some the tests could be repeated. Language, as an actual means of communication, was absent under the age of twenty months, but it must be remembered that even if a child is highly intelligent and has begun to talk well at home, he may be shy and inhibited when asked to talk to a stranger in strange surroundings.

There was a boy who walked, unaided, at the age of seven months and two days, and another who was only a few weeks slower than this. A girl had a vocabulary of two hundred words at the age of eighteen months (at four years, she can speak four languages). A boy, at the age of seven months, adored the water and could dive unaided without fear.

The list can be extended, and although it is obvious that, hardly without exception, these babies born with the assistance of decompression are advanced in every way and, what is also obvious, are bouncing with health and vitality, it must also be remembered that there is not one spastic among them, nor among the many that have since been born.

Whenever an experimental step is taken, be it in connection with man or beast, even when it can be proved that no harm is done in the taking of such a step, and that much good may, in fact, result, there is great reluctance to extend such steps by doctors not directly concerned with the original experiments. This cannot be criticised, such cautiousness is necessary, but it has the effect of slowing down scientific advance sometimes.

So far fifty mothers in this country (1965) have been helped by decompression during pregnancy and labour, but there is no wild rush on the part of obstetricians to extend this service. The apparatus itself, although very simple, is being modified, and facilities may be extended to mothers in a second teaching hospital in London, and its use is being considered, also, in a similar institution in Edinburgh. Professor Heyns feels that he should receive much support from paediatricians because they are concerned with the total health of a baby, including the preventative aspect of disease, but up till now, paediatricians have been more concerned with the treatment of illness than the prevention of disease.

The fact remains, however, that even if decompression is not the whole answer to the question of releasing the full human potential of brilliance, the method should receive urgent attention, for we cannot afford to waste even one chance in a thousand when it comes to sparing the heartache of the parents who produce a spastic child, nor should this chance be denied the child sufferer.

At the school referred to in the chapter on the physically handicapped, there is a child who cannot talk clearly, and will never walk but has, nevertheless, achieved six " O " levels. Perhaps if decompression had been used to facilitate her birth, the picture would have been different.

20

Pebble in the Lake

IN this book we have been concerned with an unique opportunity
—and also an unique problem, the opportunity for deploying the
richness of intelligence and imagination of a most vitally important
section of the community, the children who are gifted, and the
problem of recognizing them for their worth to ensure that they
will not be wasted by, for instance, withdrawal, for many do with-
draw as a result of being overlooked. If their minds do not get the
stimulation they need, there is boredom, under-achievement and
sometimes, even, a self-destructive journey into delinquency.

Wherever possible we have attempted to describe those particular
attributes of mind which, in a child, indicate that he or she is gifted.
A dictionary definition of the word " gift " emphasizes the element
of quality and it is quality of thought and personality which is the
unmistakable sign. It is almost impossible to define quality, but
perhaps we may try and, so far as quality of thought is concerned,
describe it as a combination of unusual insight and perception
which, together, amount to something fresh and enduring, something
which has an intrinsic authority so that the simplest statement or
action demands a respect which is completely out of proportion to
age. In a child, such a quality of mind is a stimulus, a joy and a
delight to all round who are " big " enough to accept such richly
colourful endowments in one so young.

These children are indispensable. The future of any country
depends upon the amount of various talent that it can draw upon
and put to creative and constructive use. This is not to imply the
denigration of other qualities which are independent of high intelligence—moral judgement and physical strength are equally neces-

sary, but these attributes alone will not lead to the achievements which will make a country important to the future of the world.

Without the gifted, that essential two percent. of the population, we cannot be assured of our future status and well-being. Many hundreds of thousands of pounds are spent every year on children who are at the bottom of the scale of intelligence, and this money is rightly being spent from motives of the greatest and most worthy humanitarianism, but surely there is even more point in spending money on children whose potential contribution is incalculable; who two thousand years ago, Plato called the guardians of " The Republic."

For our research we went to many parts of the country, from great centres of industry to the most isolated of rural communities. When the parents we interviewed, or the educationalists we spoke to learned of our particular interest, the result was sometimes astonishing. Occasionally, in fact, one would have assumed that nobody was bothered with this vitally important topic other than the very people that we had sought out. But all over the place are pockets of experiment trying to meet the needs of gifted children, yet such is the insularity of the native temperament, in addition to the lack of readily available funds for making the results public, that the groups undertaking this valuable work were often unaware of similar work being done, even in a neighbouring county.

We later refer to the American publication *The Gifted Child Quarterly* and were such a journal in existence here, publishing the results of this scattered experimental work, an enormous step forward would be made in avoiding the disastrous consequences of neglect, both nationally and in terms of human happiness.

Frequently we were asked what to do with this or that child whose gifts were striking but who was very much at sea for the lack of facilities which would extend his capabilities, academic, imaginative and practical, to the full. The gold was there in the earth, but there were too few with the ability to refine it.

Those people who are seriously concerned with the many-sided problem of sorting out the children of Gold are finally realizing that high intelligence or creativity might be the hallmark of the gifted and the manifestations most easily recognizable, but there are many other special abilities and general aptitudes which can so easily go unrecognized. In other words, endeavours are being made to study the whole child, to look for the subtleties as well as the obvious, and thereby eliminate the possibility of missing even one of such children.

To reduce the whole problem to a basic premise, one can consider the analogy of a business organization which is successful, or not, as the case may be, but whose achievements will be coloured almost entirely by the quality of the man or men at the top. A gifted child is, of course, the owner of its own priceless commodity, the encompassing richness of its mind, but to arrive at the quintessential elements of this commodity, the child has to be shown how to sort out the chaff from the wheat. Perceptive parents (the original " man " at the top) can do much to help but conflict exists even in the most ideal relationship between parent and child. The detached but kindly and stimulating teacher is the next most important " man at the top " and it is hoped that all educators will, gradually, lose what prejudices they may still possess and, over the years, allow their minds to open in the way of the most visionary of their profession. These visionaries may still be few, but their influence is growing and the situation tends to improve.

But there are still important gaps. One administrator feels that a Research Programme set up by some Local Authority is long overdue. This, he suggests, should take the form of a follow-up study over a period of ten years or so on children who were assessed as gifted at the time they began their Secondary education. There should be investigation, too, into the reasons why many gifted children fail to live up to their early promise. There should be much thought, also, with regard to the acceleration of the gifted within the ordinary school pattern which would sometimes mean jumping a class and at other times mean being one of a group of swift-moving intellectual equals.

" There are many other problems " he said, " such as the children who fail to achieve because of the poverty of their cultural background, and the lack of any tradition of learning in the family so that the child may feel out of place and does not wish to continue on a path which will take him farther and farther from his fellows."

The battle between those who wish for a continuation of the established Grammar School and those who are in favour of a far more general Comprehensive School reached its climax during the beginning of 1965. Many worthy people, and not only educationalists, were very much against the Government decision to make education " comprehensive " and for those who do not know much about the subject, but read, or watched on television the various antagonists to the scheme, a strong flavour of stigma must have emerged. The controversy is bound to continue because the very complete and " comprehensive " attitude of the new concept suggests, unless one goes carefully into the matter, that the gifted children especially will be the sufferers. This would seem to be due to the fact that, not having been " streamed " to begin with, they will be mixed up with pupils of far less intelligence than themselves, and their lessons, as a consequence, will necessarily have to be geared to the least intelligent member of each class.

The truth of the matter is different, as the work carried out by Dr. Robin Pedley shows. He is the present Director of the Institute of Education at the University of Exeter and was one of the first educationalists in the country to advocate the system. Within each class the pupils can be divided into very small groups, each under the close jurisdiction of the teacher. This leads to the next general objection, which is that teachers will simply not be able to cope with these individual groups, and here again the true picture turns out to be different from that believed by so many objectors to the system. Working in this far more individual way, the various pockets of achievement can be that much higher, and the teacher himself will be enormously stimulated by the results and enabled to teach to the maximum of *his* achievement.

Above all, the concept of the comprehensive takes the whole child into account in a way that the competitive entrance to Grammar Schools (and in many Public Schools with the Common Entrance Exam) following the 1944 Education Act, cannot possibly do. There should be less of the frantic race from examination to examination and the mental and emotional health of the pupil must, as a consequence, be vastly improved. There will be an enrichment which will extend far beyond the purely academic because the atmosphere in such a school is bound to be influenced by the worldly concerns that may be neglected in the more stringently academic pursuits of a Grammar School Education.

Perhaps most important of all, so far as the gifted child is concerned, he or she will be allowed to develop at his own pace, for this apparently permissive approach to the teaching of the gifted has been found to be the one which produces the best result.

It is now relevant to have a glimpse of what other countries of the world are doing in their efforts to recognize and cater for the gifted. In America, remembering the size of the country and the fact that standards of education differ from state to state, the problem is vast. One thing is shared, and that is the concept of the common course which to us seems like democracy run riot. How can all children with the exception of a small minority of white retarded children and a large majority of Negro children in the Southern States be expected to graduate if, by this, is meant the attainment of a high enough standard for the passing of college entrance examinations as we understand it? What is implied by this method of education is only too true in fact, and for some universities, the qualifications for entrance are so low that the gifted are not extended, become quickly bored and leave early.

Yet a great deal of experimental work with and for gifted children has been done in the United States. They have a nation-wide association for Gifted Children with its own journal and regularly hold conferences where parents, teachers, and the children themselves can get together and work things out, just as the parents of mentally retarded children and members of the Spastics Society have done in Britain.

Since the first conference on gifted children was held there in 1960, Canada is becoming more and more interested in the whole subject. Canada is a young country where there is a tradition of open-air living, pioneering and where the " mounties always get their man." It is therefore not surprising that until recently the majority of parents of gifted children tended to regard this situation they had on their hands as one of effeteness. Even the most urbanized of Canadians, one who would hardly know one end of a steer from the other, tended to consider an interest in sport to be more " manly " and therefore more desirable, and prejudices like this die hard. It is unfortunately still true that, in some parts of Canada, the gifted child cannot be secure in the knowledge that his parents are grateful and proud of the quality of his mind.

Nevertheless, the situation is changing. One or two schools have a " gifted children committee " and in consultation with the Head the child's programme is mapped out and his future planned. In some larger towns, consultants specializing in gifted children are employed by the education department, and in smaller towns a supervisor of special education will advise on such children to the various Heads, just as similar consultants would advise on the special treatment that should be accorded to the deaf or physically handicapped.

Dr. Roberto Assagioli, a Venetian, hopes to open shortly what will be the first educational centre in Italy for gifted children. He is a psychiatrist and intends to employ a method which he calls *psychosynthesis*. We have not been able to discover quite what this is (!) but the term implies a concern with the whole child, and for this one can only salute Dr. Assagioli and wish him luck with his proposed Centre for the Supergifted, which is planned to have the character of an agricultural settlement where the children can learn to live and work together, not only in academic subjects, but with their hands as well.

In a typically thorough Scandinavian way, Sweden experimented for five years before going " comprehensive " and this is particularly important for us to realize, bearing in mind the controversy which exists around the British plan to do likewise. The experiment employed the simplest of methods—Stockholm was divided into two sections, and in one of the sections, those children who were gifted were sent to the Swedish equivalent of a grammar school, while the others went to an ordinary secondary school. In the second section, all the children went to a comprehensive school. It took no more than five years to discover that the best results came from the section using the comprehensive method.

The Iron Curtain countries proclaim loudly that all children have every opportunity and all that is necessary to shine mentally is application to study. This would seem to discount all that is subtle in the human mind, but we do take our hat off to the way that children in these countries are catered for in their leisure time which is, for many, half the school day as buildings and teachers are still in extremely short supply. But the children have access to clubs which are something more than the shabby edifices containing ricketty billiard tables, pop records and warm Coca Cola that we too often lay on. This is a case where the gifted, indeed, have a chance by the acquisition of a really high degree of knowledge and skill in the things which interest them most, to enrich their lives.

In case we should seem to have placed undue emphasis on the educational aspect, it must be remembered that for nearly all, school for the majority of gifted children, until well into their adolescence, is their most important activity and their future will depend to a large extent upon their scholastic records and, even more important, the way their minds have been trained to cope with the sheerly intellectual side of the demands of their future career.

When they are not at school, children are at home and there seems to be a growing awareness that a healthy state of affairs is one which does not eliminate closer ties between the hours of schoolwork and the hours of family and social life. Parents need to be able to feel included in their children's attitude to schoolwork, and teachers need more than a thin slice of extra-didactic warmth if there is to be an effective relationship between themselves and the child.

This tie between school and home becomes more important every day because modern methods of teaching mean that, largely, the lessons are geared to the individual capacity of each child, and the old and restrictive methods (learning, for instance, by tables rather than by numbers of objects) are on their way out. But it seems that many parents are not aware of this and are anxious when they discover that their child is not learning his tables! The parents, too, need to be educated.

Parents and teachers should be part of a shared educative plan —educative in the widest sense, so that the positive relationships fostered at home can be transferred to school thus making effective teacher-pupil relationships possible, and in return the child can take home the social lessons he has learned from mixing with and adapting himself to his contemporaries.

Imaginative writers, such as Aldous Huxley and H. G. Wells, have written graphically of a future in which the intellect has developed to such an extent that we have become a race of fantastic " brains." Whether or not this will one day be the case no-one can say, nor indeed whether such a condition would be a good thing. By learning to worship the intellect we may forget the meaning of heart, and nothing could be a better exemplification of this than the terrible fate of the Western World implied by the remarkable film " Dr. Strangelove." Here we saw what the gifted mind could produce, the fantastic machines which could wipe out the world, and we saw too how the mind of a man cracked and made it possible for all of us to be eliminated by the very achievements that gifted scientists had made possible. A splendid and multi-coloured world of fantastic achievement is one thing, but what are we going to do about the minds that break and turn a power for good or political stability into the means of total destruction? Nevertheless, the recognition of potential great talent must be extended, and perhaps in the ways we discover to cater for it will also be included, one day, ways which will ensure that the face of evil in ourselves will also be recognized and, somehow, banished.

Meanwhile, the more we seek, the more we shall find. It is like the ever-widening circles that occur when a pebble is thrown into a lake, and the further the circles spread, the more complex the pattern of ripples becomes. A multi-factorial investigation dealing with the whole field of the gifted is an urgent need but, above all, we should be intent on providing the right sort of climate for them to prosper in, a climate in which they may be enriched in many ways.

Enrichment, indeed, is a major consideration in the lives of the gifted. As domestic life improves, as modern blocks of flats grow more self-contained in the amenities they offer (laundrettes, shopping centres) so the need to get beyond one's immediate environment for even the simplest necessity (walking along a few streets in order to take the sheets to the laundry) diminishes. A high percentage of television advertising shows us ways in which we can get progressively lazier. To have a button by one's hand, indeed, so that we do not even have to leave our chairs to turn on the television set is " sold " to us, by those who manufacture the buttons, as the new height of luxury which we cannot possibly afford to do without.

The gifted need stimuli, but if everything is not only brought to our doorstep, but packaged so attractively that we are influenced to buy it, what we are doing is alienating ourselves from life, and it is life that the gifted need to taste continually, rather than be divorced from it. A visit to a Cathedral does something more to one's soul than watching a collection of coloured slides being projected by a little machine that came in exchange for a hundred (or a thousand) coupons, or the tops of fifty packets of cereal!

There seems to be two factors operating consisting of those who are determined to wrap up everything we need in life-proof plastic, and those who realize that we must participate in life if we, ourselves, are to develop into complete human beings. It is through the veins of the latter that the rich red blood flows, and some of the things these people are doing for children tells us that there is still hope, if only we turn a deaf ear to the blandishments of the salesmen of all that is made to glitter without being gold.

What comes to mind immediately are the various Adventure Playgrounds now sprouting all over the place. Their very name contains the feeling of excitement that was planned to be aroused in the hearts of the youngsters who may have wanted to be part of this " adventure." To the gifted child, especially one from a culturally poor background, Adventure Playgrounds could well be the only means he has to practise his talents for creativeness and leadership, for it is the child himself who builds the structures which arise in these playgrounds, and the child too who is made to feel responsible for the " social " work he does there. He is, of course, under the guidance of a leader, but the operative word is " guidance " for all are encouraged to extend whatever gifts or aptitudes they have in this leisure-time (and pleasure-time) activity.

And what of the future? It is simply this—we must continue to do all we can for those children so they will not only be given the opportunities to develop into the sort of people they should be, but even when they achieve the careers most suited to their individual talents that they should shine in these very careers. From the academically gifted will come those suited to abstract ideas, the philosophers and the mathematicians, from the technically gifted, the engineers, the computer designers—workers who are primarily interested in seeing their thoughts translated into concrete results, the creatives will put into the world all that is beautiful and enduring and from the socially gifted, so highly aware of others in relation to themselves, will come the politicians, the sociologists, psychologists and all those who work with and for their fellow men.

It was the first duty of the rulers, in Plato's " Republic " to seek out the Children of Gold. For us to seek them out is our duty still.

BIBLIOGRAPHY

Atkinson. *Study of Student Resources in Ontario.* Ontario College of Education, University of Toronto, 1958.

Barbe, W. *The Exceptional Child.* Center for Applied Research in Education Inc., Washington D.C., 1963.

Bowlby, J. *Child Care and the Growth of Love.* Pelican Books, London, 1962.

Brumbaugh, F. *Hunter College (see Torrance—" Talent and Education ") Your Gifted Child.* Holt, Rinehart and Wiston, New York, 1959.

Burns, M. *Mr. Lyward's Answer.* Hamish Hamilton, London, 1956.

Carter, C. O. *Human Heredity.* Pelican Books, London, 1962.

Critchley, MacDonald. *Developmental Dyslexia.* Heinemann Medical Books, London, 1964.

Cruickshank, W. M. (Editor). *Education of Exceptional Children and Youth.* Prentice Hall, Englewood Cliffs, N.J., 1958.

Downing, J. *The Initial Teaching Alphabet.* Cassell, London, 1964.

Dunlop, J. M. *(see Cruickshank—" Education of Children of High Mental Ability ").*

Freehill, M. *Gifted Children.* Macmillan, New York, 1961.

Fleming, W. G. *(see Atkinson).*

Floud, J., Halsey, A. H., Martin, F. M. *Social Class and Educational Opportunity.* Heinemann, London, 1957.

Fordham, M. *The Life of Childhood.* Kegan Paul, Trench, Trubner, London, 1944.

Goodenough, F. *Exceptional Children.* Appleton Century Crofts, New York, 1956.

Gretzels, J. & Jackson, P. W. *Research Projects on The Gifted Student.* University of Chicago Press, 1960.

Creativity and Intelligence. John Wiley, London, 1963.

Havighurst, R. J., De Haan, R. F., & Stivers, E. *A survey of The Education of Gifted Children.* University of Chicago Press, 1955.

Heynes, O. S. *Abdominal Decompression*. Witwatersrand University Press, Johannesburg, 1963.

Hollingworth, L. S. *Children Above 180 I.Q.* World Book Company, Yonkers on Hudson, New York, 1942.

Jackson, B. *Streaming—An Education System in Miniature*. 1964.

Jackson, B., & Marsden, D. *Education and the Working Class*. 1962. Both published by Routledge & Kegan Paul, London.

Jaffe, A., & Jung, C. G. *Memories, Dreams and Reflections*. Collins, Routledge & Kegan Paul, London, 1963.

James, E. *Education and Leadership*. Harrap, London, 1951.

Laycock, S. R. *Gifted Children*. Copp, Clark, Vancouver, Toronto, Montreal, 1957.

Lewis, G. M. *Education of More Able Children in Grades 4, 5 and 6*. Dept. of Health, Education and Welfare, U.S.A., 1961.

Mason, A. S. *Health and Hormones*. Pelican Books, London, 1960.

Ostwalt, E. R. *The Role of Parents in the Training and Education of Mentally Superior Children*. Kent State University Bulletins, Ohio, 1957.

Parkyn, G. W. *Children of High Intelligence*. New Zealand Council for Educational Research, O.U.P., 1948.

Passow, A., Goldberg, M., Tannenbaum, A. J., French, W. *Talented Youth Project*. Bureau of Publications, Teachers' College, Columbia, 1955.

Pedley, R. *The Comprehensive School*. Pelican Books, London, 1963.

Pickard, P. M. *I Could a Tale Unfold*. Tavistock Publications, London, 1961.

Pierce, V., & Bowman, P. H. *Motivation Patterns of High and Low Achievers*. Dept. of Health, Education and Welfare, U.S.A., 1960.

Shertzer, B. (Editor). *Working With Superior Students*. Science Research Associates, Chicago, 1960.

Stafford Clark, D. *Psychiatry for Students*. Allen & Unwin, London, 1964.

Stationery Office. *Central Advisory Council for Education 15 to 18*. H.M.S.O. London, 1963.

Strang, R. *Mental Hygiene of the Gifted (see Witty, P.).*
  Psychology of Gifted Children and Youth (see Cruickshank, W.).
  Helping Your Gifted Child. E. P. Dulton, New York, 1960.
Terman, L., & Oden, M. *Genetic Studies of Genius (see Witty, P.).*
Torrance, E. P. *3rd Minnesota Conference on Gifted Children.*
  University of Minnesota Press, 1960.
  Talent and Education. University of Minnesota Press, 1960.
  Guiding Creative Talent. Prentice Hall, Englewood Cliffs, N. J.,
  1963.
Trapp, E. P., & Hummelstein, P. *Readings on the Exceptional
  Child.* Methuen, 1962.
Thurston, L. L. *Creative Talent.* Harper, New York, 1952.
Ward, V. S. *Educating the Gifted.* Chas: E. Merrill Books Inc.,
  Columbus, Ohio, 1961.
Willard, A. *Common Sense About Gifted Children.* Harper, New
  York, 1958.
Witty, P. (Editor and Contributor). *The Gifted Child.* D. C.
  Heath & Company, Boston, 1951.
Year Book of Education. (Editors: Bereday & Lawreys). *Concep-
  tions of Excellence in Education.* 1961.
  The Gifted Child. 1962. Evans, London.